WHAT EVERYONE SHOULD KNOW ABOUT ISLAM AND MUSLIMS

Suzanne Haneef

Library of Islam

Library of Congress Cataloging in Publication Data

Haneef, Suzanne
    What Everyone Should Know About Islam and Muslims
    1. Islam-United States. 2. Islam-Canada. 3. Islam-UK. I. Title
    BP67.A1M35   1979   305.6'971071   89-1406
    ISBN: 0-935782-00-1

Manufactured in the United States of America

To my beloved Lord,
the Most-Merciful and Kind,
who honored me with Islam,
I humbly dedicate this work

TABLE OF CONTENTS

TO THE READER

Perhaps you have been hearing a lot about Islam and Muslims in the news and are interested in knowing, justifiably, just what this religion is all about. Or perhaps you know some Muslims and have been stirred to curiosity about the faith they profess. Or perhaps someone you know, maybe even someone in your own family, has decided to embrace Islam. If so, this book is meant for you. Its purpose is to set forth the Islamic concepts and beliefs in a clear, understandable manner and then to give you an idea about how Muslims are supposed to live. In short, it presents a summary of the Islamic beliefs, ways of worship, qualities, values, morals, standards of conduct, and, in concrete and practical terms, the Islamic way of life.

I think you will agree with me that a religion which does not demand anything of its followers, or which leaves those who have newly entered into it more or less where they were before they embraced it, is an ineffective religion, a mere set of "beliefs" or rituals which does not affect the conduct of living.

Islam does not fit this description. For Islam is not a mere belief-system, an ideology or a religion in the usual sense in which these words are understood. Rather it is a total way of life, a complete system governing all aspects of man's existence, both individual and collective. It is in fact a religion which, as I hope to demonstrate in the course of this book, frees the human being from domination by his material and animal aspects and makes him truly human.

The meaning of the word Islam is "submission" and "peace." In the course of making an individual *muslim*—that is, one who is in a state of islam or submission to the One True God—Islam profoundly affects his thinking and behavior. Indeed, there is no aspect of a person's life, nor of the life of the society which is made up of such people, which it does not touch and transform in keeping with its basic concept, that of the Lordship and Sovereignty of God and the human being's responsibility to Him. Islam's first requirement is belief and its second action. Out of its concepts and beliefs, a certain attitude toward life, toward one's own self, toward other human beings, toward the universe; a certain kind of personality; a distinctive type of human interaction; a particular mode of worship, of family life, manners, living habits and so on in relation to all aspects of life, develops.

We live in an age of tremendous upheaval and uncertainty. People everywhere are groping anxiously for something that can save humanity, which has lost its way and is on the brink of unprecedented disaster. It may be true that today we live in an era of the ultimate in material civilization and progress, but in the realm of values and morals mankind appears to be close to bankruptcy. In the Islamic view, these problems are fundamentally of a spiritual nature, the result of the human being's having lost sight of who he is in relation to himself, to other human beings, and above all to God, in Whom being itself, and all human relationships, originate. And until he is able to find meaningful and correct answers to the ultimate questions and solutions to his problems which are compatible with the fundamental realities of existence and his own nature, his life will remain adrift without a base and without a direction, his personality will be distorted and fragmented, his human nature abused by permitting its animal part to dominate, and his societies full of overwhelming problems.

Islam claims to provide such answers and solutions, ones which are compatible with reason, logic, the realities of the physical universe, and with human nature itself. For Islam is, above all, a view of the total Reality, encompassing the existence and attributes of the Creator, the human being's relationship with

Him, his role and purpose in this world, and the relationship between this life and the life of the Hereafter, which puts all that exists into proper perspective and gives balance and direction to the life of human beings and their societies.

However, Islam is so little known and understood in the Western world that to many people, especially in America, it is simply another strange religious cult or sect. Allah is some sort of a heathen deity, Muhammad is someone who is worshiped by hordes of pagans overseas, and Muslims are either militant sword-wielding bedouins mounted on camels, fanatical men of religion with long robes and beards, or rich, decadent playboys. Indeed, Islam has been so gravely misunderstood and misrepresented in the West that many people in America and Europe think of it as an enemy to any sort of stability, peace and progress; they mistrust it, fear it and regard it as a dire threat without as a rule knowing anything about it other than what the popular media convey, which almost invariably reflects grave inaccuracies and errors.

As these lines are written, the media are full of such "news" and views about Islam and Muslims; daily one can hear or read item after item on the subject. Virtually without exception these misrepresent not only the details of the Islamic system and the motivations and characters of sincere Muslims, but also the fundamental concepts and teachings of the religion. They are often so gravely distorted that, indeed, a Muslim who encounters them may not even be able to recognize that they are concerned with the religion he has known and practiced all his life. The Western world today is full of "experts" on Islam who consider themselves far more knowledgeable about it than the Muslims who are living it day by day, but who seldom if ever take the trouble to understand Islam, especially its central world-view and basic concepts, on a deeper level.

Why is all this so? First, it is due in part to the legacy of history. Islam and Christendom confronted each other as enemies during the Crusades and afterwards, and the propaganda against the enemy and its beliefs and way of life which is common during times of conflict, whether it is true or false, has never yet been laid to rest in the Western world. Second, it is partly due to the confused and distorted picture of Islam which the behavior of many Muslims, those who profess this faith but do not live by it, often doing everything which it does not permit and doing nothing which it requires, very unfortunately presents. It is also due in part to the fact that many people in the Western world think of any religious system in terms of Christian concepts and values, or in terms of the concepts of Western civilization, which do not necessarily fit with or apply to Islam. And finally, it is also undoubtedly due to the fact that many people in the West, particularly in America, have such an unquestioning conviction of the innate superiority and rightness of the American or Western way of life that they do not consider it necessary or important to be accurately informed about others' viewpoints and ways of life. To many of us Muslims remain, "those people over there," whose only possible utility or interest is in relation to whether or not they will sell us the oil we need or boost our economy by buying our goods. We often regard them, with secret satisfaction in our own superiority as the advanced people of the West, as simple, child-like beings whose world-view must also be wrong because ours is right.

All too few people in the Western world realize that the followers of Islam constitute the second largest religious community in the world today (the first being Christianity). It is the faith professed by over one billion people living in every part of the globe, including the countries of the West, with the largest numbers concentrated in the region between North Africa and Malaysia. Hence, if for no reason other than its tremendous relevance to the contemporary world, Islam and its followers surely deserve to be represented accurately and understood correctly by anyone who desires to be well informed and aware. In addition, since today there are large numbers of people who profess Islam, both foreign-born Muslims and Western converts, living in America and in Europe where Islam is the second largest religious community at the present time, Islam also deserves to be known and understood correctly as a faith which increasingly has more and more relevance to the religious community of the Western world.

I would like, therefore, to request the reader, for the sake of fairness and objectivity as he approaches this brief study of Islam, to try his best to clear his mind of any preconceptions he may have about Islam, whether these have been gathered from the news, movies or television programs, from newspaper or magazine articles, or simply the vague, piece-meal picture of Islam and Muslims which one somehow picks up from here and there, or any combination of these. As a rule such presentations do not constitute reliable or authoritative sources of information about either Islam or Muslims and are, in fact, often the propagators of misconceptions, fallacies and prejudices rather than of accurate information. If, therefore, the reader can set aside temporarily whatever he may have gleaned from such sources concerning the subject, hopefully when he has finished reading this book (and, if he is interested, others from among the titles listed at the end of this volume) he will be in a much better position to determine what part is accurate and what part is false and misleading.

In writing this book I have been all too keenly aware that to present Islam as it should be presented is at once a great challenge and an almost overwhelming responsibility. I have undertaken this responsibility with a great sense of inadequacy for the task, for there are countless other Muslims who are far better qualified for it both in terms of their knowledge and their practice of Islam. Nonetheless, to do so has been felt as a duty. Many books about Islam are available, but virtually all of them are either by non-Muslim authors who invariably reflect many blatant distortions and prejudices against Islam or by Muslims whose writings, although they may portray Islam correctly and indeed often with great depth and meaningfulness, are not really geared to a non-Muslim, Western readership. Since I have myself, in the process of coming to an understanding of Islam, gone through the simultaneous process of asking and finding

answers to the questions which have been asked, and hopefully
answered, in this volume, I have felt an obligation to share this
understanding with others who may be interested in knowing
what Islam is or what it can offer to mankind. It is my earnest
prayer that God will accept this small effort and make it useful
for a better understanding of Islam, the path of peace and submission to Him.

The Author

PART ONE:
BELIEFS AND
ACTS OF WORSHIP

I.

BELIEFS

THE ISLAMIC CREED

"*La ilaha illa Llah, Muhammadun rasool Allah*" — "There is no deity except God, Muhammad is the Messenger of God."

This simple statement of a Muslim's basic beliefs is the starting point for all that follows. From this expression of belief in the Oneness and Uniqueness of God and the messengership of Muhammad stem all of Islam's concepts, attitudes, moral values and guidelines for human behavior and relationships. How can all this follow from this one simple and seemingly quite obvious statement?

The first part of this declaration, "*La ilaha illa Llah*," attests not only to the Oneness and Uniqueness of God, the Deity. It signifies, at the same time, the oneness of the lordship, the sovereignty and the authority in the universe and this world. For when we affirm that there is no deity except the One God, we are actually stating that as there is no other Creator and Sustainer of the universe, this world and all that is in them, there can likewise be no other Ruler, Law Giver and Supreme Authority for mankind. God, the Lord of all creation, creates what He pleases, giving each of His creations the nature, function and role which He desires for it; in this He is accountable to no one. All things are under His absolute control. The purpose for which He created

3

human beings is to acknowledge, worship and obey Him alone, and at the same time to manage the affairs of this world and administer it with justice and righteousness according to His all-wise laws.

How do we know all this? How can a mere human being, a very limited and finite creature know about God—that is, about Infinity and His purposes for mankind, the answers to the multitude of basic questions which encompass God's nature and attributes, the human being's relationship to Him, and why he has been put into this world? We are living in an era in which we have increasingly lost the conviction of the meaning and purpose of existence; indeed, the entire complex of modern civilization seems to proclaim the utter purposelessness and meaninglessness of life. Then how can we know?

Indeed, these are the most vital and basic questions for any human being. Without satisfactory answers to them, life makes no sense. It has neither purpose nor meaning, and one is simply going through the motions of living without any reason other than the fact that he happens to be alive. Hence the essential task facing each individual is to search for the answers to these questions until he finds them and, when he has found them, to acknowledge their truth and to live by them as faithfully as he can. But the question remains: Where are the answers to them to be found?

Assuredly, if (as many people believe) religion were simply a device invented by the human being to explain the world of nature or for ordering human affairs, human beings would have been able to arrive at satisfactory answers to these questions through their own reasoning and observation and to guide their lives by them in a suitable manner: the worship of the forces of nature, spirits and demons, sticks and stones and gods made by human hands and mythological figures connected to the world of men by their semi-human nature represents various efforts on their part to do so throughout the course of history. But to arrive at the objective truth. at a correct knowledge of the meaning and purpose of existence, the nature and attributes of the Creator of all things, and of the human being's role and ultimate destiny, by the human being's unaided efforts is an obvious impossibility since it concerns what is totally outside the realm of human observation or deductive faculties; even if some individuals should, by their own efforts succeed at grasping some part of these truths, they would have no certain or positive means of verifying them.

The only possible means by which human beings can have access to an unquestionably correct understanding of such matters is if the Source of everything, the willing, acting, sustaining Power Whom we call God, Himself imparts this knowledge to us by whatever means He may deem fit. And this is precisely the significance of the second part of Islam's declaration of faith, "*Muhammadun rasool* Allah"—Muhammad is the Messenger of God.

Since the dawn of true human consciousness, Islam asserts, the Creator not only implanted in human beings the awareness of His existence, the innate knowledge that there is a non-corporeal, transcendent Being Who created them and the world around them,[1] He also provided them with the answers to these vital questions which have occupied their minds since their emergence as thinking. questioning, problem solving beings on this planet, conveying His guidance to humankind through various individuals whom He chose as His message-bearers to different groups of people to be the connecting link between Himself and the human being, so to speak. Through the passing of time and changes occasioned by human error, much of the message which they brought was lost. However, enough remains of the earlier scriptures or the teachings of earlier messengers—of the revelations entrusted by God to such prophets as Abraham, Moses, Jesus and many others (God's peace and blessings be on them all)—to make it very clear that this Message has been basically one and the same throughout history: that there is a single, unique Being Who is the Lord and Master of all creation; that this Being has made laws to govern the conduct of human beings; and that each individual is accountable to this Being for how he lives his life.

Thus Islam does not claim to be a new religion. Rather it is the original religion, that primordial faith which has had its roots deep in human consciousness since the first true human being walked upon earth because the Creator Himself implanted it there, the faith revealed to and preached by all the prophets: the religion of submission and accountability to the One God. Islam teaches the divine origin of this message, pointing to the similarity and continuity of the teachings brought by the various messengers of God throughout history, but it makes it clear that in the course of time they were changed and grave distortions appeared among them. Hence the divine origin of these messages is to be believed in but not necessarily their present form or contents since their present condition makes it impossible to determine what part of them has been changed, either accidentally or deliberately by the hands of people.

Each one of the prophets was a man like other men, with the same human needs and feelings; Islam most emphatically denies any suggestion of the divinity or super-human nature of God's messengers. At the same time, they were men of special qualities whom God singled out from the rest of humanity for the task of conveying His guidance. The prophets are characterized by their total submission to God and their nearness to Him, their pure and upright natures, the extraordinary righteousness of their conduct, and their unruling commitment to the mission with which they were entrusted.

The guidance revealed suited the mentality and needs of the particular peoples to whom it was addressed. Consequently many earlier prophets were sent with miracles and signs since the people of their eras, whose belief in God was very weak or altogether lacking, were willing to acknowledge Him only when His existence and power were demonstrated by such proofs. At length, when the mind of the human being had developed to its full potential. God raised His last prophet, Muhammad, an Arab descended from Abraham, with the final and complete statement of His guidance for all time to come. And it is because Muslims follow the guidance which was conveyed through Muhammad (may God's peace and blessings be on him), the guidance which carries the complete and final proclamation of God's laws and commands for humankind, that *"Muhammadun rasool* Allah"—

Muhammad is the Messenger of God—is so significant and vital as to form the second part of the Muslims statement of faith.

Far from being a state of degradation and servility, the human individual's exclusive submission to the Creator alone invests him with greatness and sublimity, for by means of it he is freed from obeying and serving anything less than God, the only Being Who can ever be worthy of his devotion and obedience. *"La ilaha illa Llah, Muhammadun Rasool Allah"* is therefore that powerful statement of faith which represents the liberation of the one who professes it from servitude and submission to anything or anyone other than God Most High. It is the denial of all other claimants to divinity and supreme authority, the affirmation of God's Oneness and Sovereignty, and the statement of belief in and acceptance of His guidance as revealed to Prophet Muhammad (peace be on him), the last of God's messengers.

THE ISLAMIC VIEW OF REALITY

Every human being who comes into the world must deal, at one level or another, with the question of what constitutes Reality. Consciously or otherwise, each one of us lives with his own individual understanding of what makes up the totality of existence. This reality concept determines to a great extent how we relate to the universe, our comprehension of the purpose of our existence, and what role we play in this world.

Is the physical universe—what we can see, touch, measure or perceive with our faculties or instruments—all there is, or is there something more? Where did we come from, and where do we go from here? Is it all the result of blind chance and randomness, or is it part of a purposeful, meaningful scheme and plan? Is there Someone in charge of it all Who is Himself the Ultimate Reality or not? Does the human being's life itself have any reason or ultimate significance, or is the human being just a perishable physical entity who will cease to exist like all other living things? Is this life the only life, or will it be followed by some other state of existence, and if so, of what kind?

In fact, an individual's conception of Reality—his answers to these and many other related questions—is nothing less than his basic orientation to the universe, his perception of his place and the role he is to play in it. Upon this conception rests, in effect, all that a human being is and strives to become, his relationship with himself, with others and with the world around him, and above all, with his Creator.

At this time in history many people are asking: "Is there really Anyone out there or not? And if there is, does it really matter?" Such questions are a mirror of the modern person's total alienation from himself and from his Source, and, as a result, from the universe and his fellow human beings as well. The technology oriented, mechanized environment of the Western world has trained many people to disbelieve in what is termed "the supernatural," even though they may profess to believe in God. Science, one of the greatest of present-day deities, has taught us to regard as having reality only that which can be seen, observed, measured or perceived through our senses, mental capacities or inventions. Consequently, while many people in the Western world today may not absolutely deny the existence of what they are unable to perceive, in practice they often act as if it does not exist by ignoring it altogether, or feeling that even if it does exist it has no relevance or importance in the scheme of things. Although many people profess to "believe" in God, this is often a static belief, a mere opinion that God exists rather than that He does not exist which has no significant practical consequences and does not in any affect the way they live their lives.

Others do believe, and very strongly in the "supernatural." However, their beliefs are incomplete and unreliable, depending largely on guesswork. The accuracy and validity of such beliefs cannot in any way be depended upon since they are based on ones own or others' subjective experiences; hence they cannot be taken seriously as a means of gaining accurate knowledge of the ultimate Reality of existence, especially of God as the Center and Source of that Reality, nor as constituting valid guidance for the living of life. The current preoccupation with extrasensory phenomena may be a step in the direction of acceptance of a Reality greater than the physical universe, but it consists largely of speculation coupled with the attempt to subject non-material phenomena to scientific analysis which must, in the long run, due to the nature of the material under study, be self-defeating; moreover, it cannot by any means address itself to the question of God's nature or attributes, or even His existence. That many psychic phenomena are related to and inspired by satan rather than being spiritual experiences connected to God seems a strong probability, and hence such phenomena are a very uncertain and risky foundation for either beliefs or for living.

Islam deals in a clear, straightforward manner with all these issues. In fact, Islam itself poses the questions asked above and many more, insisting that meaningful answers to them, compatible with the observed phenomena of the universe and with reason, must be sought by anyone who possesses a mind.

There is a realm of existence, Islam proclaims, which is not accessible to human sense or awareness nor bound by the limitations of the human intellect. This realm, which is beyond the human being's perception, is termed *al-ghaib*, that is, the Hidden or Unseen, while that which is known and perceptible is termed *ash-shahadah*, the Evident or Witnessed. And in Islam belief in this unseen realm is a prerequisite for belief in and understanding of God and of that part of His creation which the human being's senses and faculties cannot perceive but which is nonetheless of fundamental importance to his existence. The section which follows, concerning Islam's articles of faith, deals with these Unseen Realities.

Islam asserts that what is visible and perceptible to human faculties—*ash-shahadah*—is only a part, and perhaps a very small and insignificant part, of the totality of what exists. Although the human being cannot grasp the totality of existence, this does not in any way negate the reality of more than he is able to grasp any more than, say, an ant or an elephant can determine the totality of what exists on the basis of its limited experiences and perceptions. The fact, which it is often strangely painful for many of us to admit, is simply that the human being is a quite finite, limited being with faculties and understanding which are equipped to take in and comprehend just so much and no more. Yet the "more" is there nevertheless, that wider Reality, the totality of which is known only to its Creator.

For the existence of this wider Reality, although it cannot be perceived directly, is much evidence which is known to us all. Among these is the physical universe itself, which speaks in endless volumes about the unimaginable power, wisdom and creativity of God. The human being is another striking evidence. He comes from somewhere, from non-being into being, and when he dies it is obvious that the most vital part of him is gone. In his spiritual feelings and aspirations, too, the human being's longing for something deeper and higher than the material sphere, there are clear intimations of the existence of a non-material realm of the greatest importance, to which the human being is in some unknown way so intimately bound up that to ignore or reject it must inevitably result in very serious consequences to the individual and his society. Religious feelings, expressions and movements are common to all human beings, and many of them possess similar features and characteristics. In particular, the great monotheistic religions—Judaism, Christianity and Islam—demonstrate very striking similarities, pointing unmistakably to their common origin in the same Source, God Most High. And finally, various extrasensory phenomena, among which we may include dreams and premonitions relating to future events and many other striking manifestations of the existence of a non-material realm, provide us with some dramatic clues concerning the Unseen Reality.

In Islam, God is the center of that Reality; indeed, He is the Reality. God is the One Who does everything, the Creator and Sustainer of all that exists, the Provider of all things with their sustenance. He is the Alternator of night and day, the One Who creates what He wills in the wombs of the mothers, Who renews the earth after it is dead and brings out of it, by means of rain from the sky and nourishment within the ground, the growing things which constitute food for human beings and beasts. And it is He Who gives a term of life to His creatures as He sees fit. It is He Who will bring forth the bodies of human beings from their graves and join them to their souls on that awesome day, concerning which there is no doubt, when He will bring the universe to an end, and it is He Who will judge them according to the most absolute and impartial standards of justice and mercy. He is the

Supreme, the Irresistible, the All-Knowing and the All-Wise, the One Who is accountable to no one but to Whom all things are accountable, Who does what He wills with His creation, and before Whom all things bow in submission, and at the same time He is also the Merciful, the Gracious, the Loving and the Forgiving.

This is Islam's view of Reality, the view of Reality held by countless Muslims throughout the world. Such concepts form a vital part of the Muslim's consciousness, beginning in early childhood. He grows up with the awareness of God's reality and power, His beneficence and kindness to His creation: with the realization that this life is only a very small part of a Reality so vast that the mind of a human being cannot conceive of it except in an extremely limited manner; and with the knowledge that it is not the final stage of his existence, but a continuous one, as there was a time when, in the words of the Quran, the human being was "*a thing not (even) mentioned.*" (76:1) God brought him out of non-being into existence: from a sperm and an egg in the bodies of his parents into an embryo growing in his mother's womb, then into independent life when he was born into the world; from helpless infancy into childhood, and from maturity into old age during which he becomes like a weak, helpless child all over again: and from thence into another life which will be the final state of all human beings. In that life, those who acknowledged God as their Lord, followed His guidance and strove to please Him will be in a condition of enduring happiness and felicity beyond the capacity of the human mind to imagine, while those who denied Him and devoted themselves to deities other than God, rejecting His guidance and living for themselves or for their lusts and passions, will be in an unimaginably fearful state of agony and torment in keeping with the state of their own souls.

Islam also proclaims that human nature has its own reality. While various Western philosophies or theories concerning the human being conceive of him as a glorified machine, a being who reacts mechanically as "programmed" by his emotions, environment or biochemical processes, or, conversely, as a higher kind of animal, the Islamic conception is very different. Such materialistic approaches are seen as extremely false, misleading representations of the true nature of the human being. For the human being, Islam asserts, is a unique creation of God's possessing an obvious, outward aspect—the physical body—and a hidden, inner aspect—the mind, emotions and soul. The uniqueness of the human being's nature lies in the fact that he has been endowed with freedom of choice and judgment between right and wrong, capacities for thinking, transmitting knowledge, feeling and acting which have not been given to other creatures, and an immortal soul which lives on after the death of the physical body. Thus the human being is a composite of many aspects, levels and functions, the totality of which represents the reality of human nature.

God has created the human being with this complex and multi-faceted nature, Islam asserts, not so that there may be war and strife between the various elements but in order that they may form a smoothly functioning, harmonious whole. This in itself constitutes the great task, the ultimate challenge of being human. Each element of the human being's nature has its role and function, its legitimate needs and right to satisfaction; but in order to bring about the harmony which God intends among them, the individual must exercise the power of his will and govern them according to the laws which God has laid down for his well-being, thus achieving synthesis, integration and balance within his personality. This is why Islam concerns itself not merely with "religious" and "spiritual" matters but with all aspects of human life, all of which fall within the framework of religion in the Islamic sense of the term, treating the human being as an indivisible, organic whole in keeping with the reality of his uniquely human nature.

Such a correct understanding of the human being's true nature and his place in the scheme of things is of vital importance in the Islamic framework. By means of God's guidance conveyed through the prophets, the human being has been shown how the reality of his nature fits into the total Reality and has been informed what is expected of him in relation to that Reality, the center and focus of which is God Most High. In this way he will be able to live in harmony and balance rather than in conflict and chaos during his brief journey from one phase of this Reality this earthly life—to the next, that is, the enduring life of the Hereafter, thereby achieving true worth and true success both in this world and in the world-to-come.

THE ARTICLES OF FAITH[2]
GOD (ALLAH)

"Say (O Muhammad): 'He is God. the One, the Self-Sufficient. He begets not nor is He begotten, and there is none like Him.'" (112:1-4)

"Whatever is in the heavens and on earth glorifies God, for He is the Mighty, the Wise. To Him belongs the dominion of the heavens and the earth. It is He Who gives life and death, and He has power over all things. He is the First and the Last, the Evident and the Immanent, and He has full knowledge of all things. It is He Who created the heavens and the earth in six days (stages or eons), and is moreover firmly established on the throne (of authority). He knows what enters into the earth and what comes forth from it, and what descends from the heavens and what mounts up to it: and He is with you wherever you may be. And God sees all that you do. To Him belongs the dominion of the heavens and the earth. and all affairs are referred back to God. He merges night into day and He merges day into night. And He has full knowledge of what is in the hearts (of people)." (57:1-6)

Let us now look further at the Islamic conception of God, the first of Islam's fundamental articles of faith. To what extent does it resemble the conceptions of God taught by other religions and in what way is it unique and different?

In the Islamic view, His attributes are those of one Who is above any sort of limitations, such as having a beginning or an end, begetting or being begotten, or requiring food, rest or pro-creating; for He is the One Who gives such dimensions and attributes to His creatures, while He Himself does not share them in the slightest degree. The Quran says:

> *"God is He than Whom there is no other deity. He knows the Unseen (al-ghaib) and the Evident (ash-shahadah). He is the Merciful, the Compassionate. God is He than Whom there is no other deity—the Sovereign, the Holy One, the Source of Peace, the Guardian of Faith, the Preserver of Safety, the Mighty, the Irresistible, the Supreme. Glory be to God! (high is He) above the partners they attribute to Him. He is God, the Creator, the Evolver, the Bestower of Forms. To Him belong the most beautiful names. Whatever is in the heavens and on earth glorifies Him, and He is the Mighty, the Wise."* (59:22.24)

One who ponders over the nature of God with an open mind in relation to the observed facts of the universe has no choice but to realize that He cannot, by definition, be simply a sort of super-man Who sits above the clouds and directs affairs while sharing in creaturely needs and attributes. For God is nothing less than the Originator and Fashioner of the universe with all its vast and perfect systems, the One Who sustains and keeps it functioning according to His infinitely wise plans and laws. And thus it is clear and certain as Islam emphatically proclaims that He is infinitely beyond anything which the mind or senses of the human being can grasp or comprehend or imagine or explain, and that He is far, far above having any similarity to any of His creation. For He alone is the Creator and everything else is the created: He alone is divine, and no human being or any other creature can ever share His divinity or His unique attributes as Creator and Sustainer in the slightest degree. In short, God Most High has not the least resemblance to the limited, petty gods with their semi-human nature which the minds of men, due to their imperfect knowledge and understanding, have invented to supply the deficiencies in their comprehension but who, at the same time, fall so short of being God-like. His divine nature is entirely unique and can be grasped only through the contemplation of His attributes and His creation. The Quran says:

> *"God! There is no deity except Him, the Living, the Eternal. No slumber can overpower Him nor sleep. His are all things in the heavens and on earth. Who is there who can intercede in His presence except as He permits? He knows what is before them and what is hidden from them, and they cannot comprehend anything of His knowledge except what He wills His kingdom spreads over the heavens and the earth, and the guarding of them does not weary Him, and He is the Exalted, the Almighty."* (2:255)

Yet God's existence does not have the least relevance for mankind if He is not actively concerned with His creation, or if (as some people imagine) He created the universe and the human being and then went off and forgot about them, leaving them on their own to sink or swim. But Islam proclaims that God is the Reality, and thus His existence has absolute relevance and meaning for every single human being since it is solely in relation to God that we exist and move through the journey of this life on our way back to Him. Islam, then, asserts that God is always active and is concerned and creatively involved with every single part of His creation, from the vastest of stars down to the very atoms which comprise them, with every part of its macro- and micro-systems, and that it exists, continues and fulfills its functions by His command and will. For His concern is not merely in creating but also in sustaining, directing and guiding: in providing for His creations—maintaining, ordering and regulating them, and, in respect to human beings, in giving them the direction necessary for living their lives in this world in such a manner as will ensure their everlasting good in the life-to-come.

God is not concerned with the human being, however, as the sole or necessarily the most important of His creations, but as the one creature on earth (which is only one part of His unimaginable vast and complex creation) whom He has endowed with a thinking mind, a feeling heart, the ability to store and transmit knowledge, and to whom He has given freedom of choice. At the same time, God asks the human being to use this freedom of choice to voluntarily and deliberately choose what God wants for him rather than to follow his own random and often chaotic desires: that is, to submit his will to God's higher will and by this means to carry out the responsibilities, both personal and collective, which God has entrusted to him. For not only does the Creator have the absolute right to make whatever rules or laws He sees fit for His creatures, but He also has the absolute right to their obedience. At the same time, He alone possesses the all-embracing, absolute knowledge and wisdom to provide His creatures with such guidance as will lead to their assured well-being both in this world and in the Hereafter.

Such a belief in God and the human being's relationship to Him, however, is for the conscientious Muslim no mere intellectual exercise. For as he believes that God alone is the Master of the universe, the Lord of men, the sole Authority and Legislator, and that the human being is nothing but a humble slave before Him, it follows that there must be no other lords and authorities in his life besides God. Islam proclaims that all other elements which claim the human being's obedience and devotion, and which attempt to rule or dominate his life, are false and are in competition with God for lordship over him. It insists that one who truly and wholeheartedly believes that God alone is the sole and rightful Sovereign and Law Giver must not and will not obey or give his devotion or allegiance to other claimants to authority and sovereignty. Rather he must reject them all, submit himself to God alone, and strive with all his energies against the domination of deities other than God.

A little thought will make it clear that no matter how free an individual may consider himself to be, nevertheless he submits to some authority, his life is oriented around some goal, and his loyalty and devotion are given to someone or something. Every single one of us submits to and worships some deity which holds sway over our hearts. Either this deity is God Himself or it is, in every case without exception. something lesser than God since everything is lesser than He. Such a deity may be a human being such as a ruler, religious figure, philosopher or a member of one's family: it may be some man made ideology, philosophy or -ism. Such worship may be taking "productivity," "progress," "work," or "the state" as one's idol: it may be love of self, pride in family, descent, race, education, occupation, health, status or intelligence: it may be catering to one's own desires and becoming enslaved by them. Or it may be deifying science or the arts, or becoming the slave of fads and fashions, pleasures and lusts and passions, personal habits or the demands of society, or any of the thousand-and-one deities of the human being's own invention which are known to all of us, which effectively replace the lordship of God Most High over our hearts and lives.

We have spoken of the human being's attribute of freedom of choice. But this does not apply simply to the various single decisions which one makes every day of his life in matters big and small. Such choices depend, in fact, upon the basic, central choice which one makes to direct the whole of his existence. The greatest and most fundamental choice which every human being is called upon to make is to decide who is his Lord, for whom he lives his life, to whom is his goal, and who he worships, serves and obeys. Indeed, Islam emphatically proclaims, the choice is between only two possible ways: to be in bondage to human ideas and notions and desires, or to consciously and voluntarily commit oneself to be bound by the standards, criteria and laws of God alone; to be the slave of human masters, living by man-made values philosophies and doctrines, or to be the slave of the true Master of men, God the Praised and Exalted; to be satisfied to live and work for something lesser, or to dedicate oneself to living and striving for the only One Who can be worthy of such devotion from a human being, the only One Who can truly guide and give meaning to the human being's life, Almighty God alone.

In Western society today we hear a great deal of talk about "freedom." Such freedom, Islam asserts, is in reality enslavement: enslavement to one's own ego or to other human beings or their ideas and values. And all enslavement to anything or anyone other than God Most High is enslavement to something which is not worthy to be the master of a human being, for only the Exalted Creator and Sustainer of the universe can be worthy of occupying this place in the life of one who has been made (as the Quran states) superior even to the angels. True freedom does not consist of license to do whatever one wants while being the slave of one's own particular deity; rather freedom consists of being free from enslavement to anything or anyone other than one's real Master. Islam's unique task is thus to liberate the human being from enslavement and servitude to anything other than God, and to free him to worship and serve Him alone.

> *"Say (O Muhammad), 'Verily, my prayer and my worship, my life and death, are for God, the Lord of the worlds. He has no associate (in His divinity). This I am commanded, and I am the first of those who submit.' Say: 'Shall I seek for a lord other than God when He is the Lord of all things?' Every soul draws the earning (of its acts) on none but itself. No bearer of burdens can hear the burden of another. In the end you will all return to God: then He will tell you about that concerning which you differed. It is He Who has made you vicegerents of the earth and has raised some of you above others in rank so that He may test you in what He has given you. Indeed, your Lord is swift in punishment, yet He is indeed the Forgiving, the Merciful."* (6:162-165)

THE ANGELS

> *"But verily over you are protectors (angels), kind and honorable, writing down (your deeds)."* (82:10-11)

> *"He sends down His angels with inspiration of His command to such of His servants as He pleases, (saying), 'Warn (the human being) that there is no god but I, so do your duty to Me.'"* (16:2)

> *"The Messenger believes in what has been sent down to him from his Lord, as do the people of faith. Each one (of them) believes in God, His angels, His scriptures and His messengers . . . ."* (2:285)

Belief in the existence of beings called angels is common to various faiths. It is also a fundamental belief of Islam. But what, in the Islamic frame of reference, are angels?

It is obvious that God, the All-Mighty, the All-Knowing, is able to create any kinds of creatures He pleases. As we can see within our world alone, He has indeed created an enormous variety of creatures of all sorts, with very different natures, functions and appearance, among which are some beings possessing intelligence. The Holy Quran makes it clear that men are not the only intelligent beings created by God.[3] Another order of intelligent beings are angels, who act as God's agents and serve Him in many ways. They are created of light and unlike human beings and *jinn* have not been endowed with free will. Thus they are absolutely obedient to God's commands and are engaged in worship and service to Him. They are sent to protect people, to administer God's punishments, to carry His messages, and to perform various other functions. Human beings cannot as a rule see or hear angels, but they are present in our world nevertheless, carrying out the various duties assigned to them by their Creator. Each human individual is attended by two angels who record all his deeds up to the moment of his death in an account which will be presented to him on the day of judgment, the accuracy of which he will not be able to deny.

Because the glory and majesty of the Creator is so awesome and overwhelming that a limited, flesh-and-blood human being is unable to bear direct contact with Him, God chose to convey His revelation to the prophets, including Muhammad (God's peace and blessings be on them all) through the agency of an angel.[4] The name of this honored angelic messenger is Gabriel (Jibreel in Arabic).[5] It is because of this vital role of angels as bringers of the divine revelation to the prophets that belief in them is so important as to form a fundamental article of faith in Islam.

THE REVEALED SCRIPTURES

"And before this was the Scripture of Moses as a guide and a mercy. And this Scripture (the Quran) confirms it in the Arabic tongue, to warn the wrong-doers and as a glad tidings to those who do good." (46:12)

"And in their footsteps We[6] sent Jesus the son of Mary . .

> . . *We gave him the Injeel[7]; therein was guidance and light, and confirmation of what is in hand of the Torah[8], a guidance and an admonition to those who fear God."* (5:46)

> *"It is He Who revealed to you (Muhammad) the Scripture (the Quran) in truth confirming what is in hand of (the Scriptures) that went before it. And He revealed the Torah and the Injeel before this as guidance to mankind. And He revealed the criterion (of judgment between right and wrong) . . . ."* (3:3-4)

Belief in the reality of God's guidance to mankind in the form of revealed books or scriptures is another basic article of belief in Islam.

We have already discussed the Islamic teachings concerning the oneness and continuity of the divine guidance throughout the human history, that guidance which only the One Who possesses absolute knowledge of all things could provide for His creatures. However, the guidance revealed to all the prophets before Muhammad (peace be on them all) was sent to particular groups of people; it was not intended to be universal because humanity had not yet reached the stage of readiness for such a final, comprehensive statement of God's guidance for all time to come. This is clear from what the Quran states concerning the messages given to various prophets, from what the Old Testament says concerning them, and from the statement attributed to Jesus that "I was sent only to the lost sheep of the house of Israel." (Matthew 15:24)

The final link in the chain of revealed scriptures. Islam asserts, is the Holy Quran. Quran is an Arabic word meaning "recitation" or "reading." It was revealed to the Prophet (peace be on him) over a period of twenty-three years during the interval between his fortieth year and his death in numerous parts which bore an intimate relationship to the events through which the Prophet and his community, the first Muslims, were passing at the time. As we have mentioned, it was communicated to him through the agency of the angel Gabriel. The angel appeared to the Prophet on frequent occasions in his true angelic form or in the form of a man during intense states of inner concentration which were at times observed and documented by the Prophet's Companions and family members: they have left behind for posterity a clear account, which is confirmed by the Prophet's own narratives, of how the revelations came to him.

The Quran speaks in powerful, moving language of the attributes of God, His immense power and creativity, of the human being's relationship and responsibility to Him, and of the certainty of the coming of the last day and the life hereafter. It lays down moral and ethical principles to govern all aspects of human life, both individual and collective, as well as practical guidelines for various types of human interaction. It also narrates the histories of some of the earlier prophets and peoples as an example and encouragement to the Prophet and his community and as a warning to those who deny God. Its main theme, reiterated over and over in powerful terms, is the reality of God's existence and supreme power, the purposefulness of His creation and of all that occurs, and the human being's position as God's slave, His steward and vicegerent who is accountable to Him in everything.

The Holy Quran is the only divinely-revealed scripture in the history of mankind which has been preserved to the present time in its exact original form. For although parts of earlier revelations, such segments of the Torah given to Moses, the Psalms revealed to David, and the Evangel revealed to Jesus still remain, they are so heavily intermixed with human additions and alterations that it is very difficult to determine what part of them constitutes the original message (as many Biblical scholars admit only too readily), much less to guide one's life by them. That the Quran has been preserved in the exact Arabic wording in which it was revealed to Prophet Muhammad (peace be on him) and in the exact order in which he himself placed it as commanded by divine revelation, is a matter well-documented historically and beyond dispute.

Because it is the word of God, the Quran is always recited in Arabic, the language in which it was revealed, in the Islamic prayers (*salah*) and on other occasions, never in translation. However, it may certainly be read for understanding in translation by those who do not know Arabic, together with a commentary if desired. Nevertheless, because of its extremely distinctive style and language, it is impossible for a translation to do more than convey its bare meaning. The great nobility of its form of expression, the earnest, moving, eloquent style which is its outstanding characteristic, cannot be translated, and hence any translation must be regarded (as all translators themselves confirm) as a mere approximation to the sense of the words. While Islam does not rest on miracles or signs and wonders as some other religions do, many who are familiar with the highest in Arabic literary style regard the Quran itself as a miracle, so unparalleled is its language and form of expression. Indeed, the Quran itself contains a challenge to the unbelievers of Muhammad's time to try to produce a piece of writing comparable to it, and while many tried during his time to compose something similar to it, no one could succeed in doing so. To one conversant with Arabic, the divine origin of the Quran can be readily grasped by comparing Muhammad's language (of which thousands of word-for-word examples are recorded) with the language of the Quran, which is the word of God. The one is ordinary language of an Arab of his time, while the other is language of such a sublime and exalted quality as no human being has ever been able to approximate either then or since. We will have to say more concerning the divine origin of the Quran under the next topic, the messengers of God.

> *"And if you (the unbelievers) are in doubt as to what We have revealed to Our servant (Muhammad), then produce a surah (chapter of the Quran) like it, and call your witnesses besides God if you are truthful. And if you cannot and you cannot then fear the fire (of hell) whose fuel is men and stones, which awaits those who reject faith."* (2:23-24)

> *"This is the Scripture in which there is no doubt. In it is guidance for the God-conscious, who believe in the unseen,*

and are steadfast in prayer (salah), and spend (in charity) out of what We have provided for them; and those who believe in what was revealed to you (Muhammad) and in what was revealed before you, and are certain of the hereafter. These are on (the way of) guidance from their Lord, and these are they who will be successful." (2:2-5)

"But most of them follow only conjecture. Indeed, conjecture does not avail anything against the truth. Verily, God knows what they do. And this Quran cannot be produced by anyone other than God. Rather it is a confirmation of that which is in hand (of earlier scriptures) and a fuller explanation of the Scripture (God's revelations to mankind throughout the ages) wherein there is no doubt from the Lord of the worlds." (10:36 37)

THE MESSENGERS OF GOD

"For assuredly We sent among every people a messenger (with the command), 'Serve God and shun wickedness.' Of them were some whom God guided and of them were some on whom error became inevitably (established). So travel through the earth and see what was the end of the deniers (of truth)." (16:36)

"Say (O Muslims): 'We believe in God and in what is revealed to us, and in what was revealed to Abraham and Ishmael and Isaac and Jacob and the Tribes (of Israel), and in what was given to Moses and Jesus and in what was given to the prophets from their Lord. We make no distinction between any of them (in believing them all to be God's messengers) and to Him do we submit ourselves." (2:136, also 3:84-85)

The messengers or prophets of God have already been discussed briefly. It is important to note here that the Islamic conception of the role and function of prophethood differs somewhat from that of Judaism and Christianity. In Islam the word "prophet" (*nabi* in Arabic) does not in any way signify one who prophesies future events. Rather it denotes one who is very near to God through the total surrender of his entire being to Him and who receives revelations from Him which constitute a source of guidance for men. If the revelation is in the form of a written scripture, the prophet is in addition a "messenger" (*rasool*) as well. All the prophets who preceded Muhammad (may God's peace and blessings be on them all) were sent with a message of warning and guidance to a particular people. None of their messages were intended to be universal, including that of Jesus, who was commissioned by God specifically as a prophet to the Children of Israel, until the last messenger, Muhammad (God's peace and blessings be on him) was entrusted with the final and complete statement of God's guidance for the whole of humanity for all time to come.

Who were some of the prophets of God? The Quran states that God sent a warner and guide to every people and it mentions the names of many of them. At the beginning of the line was Adam (Adam in Arabic, the first human being). Adam and his wife Eve (Hawwa), originally in a state of primal innocence, exercised the human attribute of freedom of choice and disobeyed God's command. Through this they learned the hard lesson of the consequence of disobedience to the divine command in the loss of their innocent state and life of peace and tranquillity. But, the Quran states, they repented and God forgave them. He then bestowed prophethood upon Adam, giving him guidance for himself and his descendants.

The first true human beings on earth were thus believers in the One God, submitting to His guidance. But gradually over a period of time their accurate perception of Reality deteriorated and they became animists or idolaters, until God raised a new messenger among them to recall them to the truth. The Quran mentions Noah (Nuh), who brought a message of warning and the need for reform to his totally corrupted people. When they refused to take heed, God destroyed them in the flood. The next major prophet whose history is narrated in the Quran is Abraham (Ibrahim). Although he grew up among idolaters, he reasoned out the folly of believing in the divinity of any finite thing, especially of those made by human hands. He surrendered himself to God with such total submission that God made him an example for people of all times. The Quran calls him "*muslim*," and so indeed all the prophets were *muslim*—that is, those who submit themselves to God alone.

From Abraham came a long line of prophets through his two sons, Ishmael (Isma'il) and Isaac (Ishaq). Ishmael was the progenitor of the Arab peoples and Muhammad (peace be on him) was among his descendants. From Isaac came a number of prophets, including his son Jacob (Yaqoob), his grandson Joseph (Yusuf), Moses (Musa), David (David), Solomon (Sulayman), John the Baptist (Yahya) and Jesus (Isa). Of these, Moses, David and Jesus (God's blessings and peace be on them) brought written scriptures revealed by God, although today only scattered portions of the originals remain, intermixed with what people have added, as is clear from an objective study of the format and content of the Biblical text.

Islam asserts that Jesus was one in the line of prophets sent to the Children of Israel. The Message he brought reiterated the necessity of submission to God and obedience to His law given through Moses, emphasizing purity of heart and sincerity of intention instead of mere formalism and empty adherence to ritual. The Quran states, as does the Bible, that Jesus was born of a virgin mother by the power of God. However, this in no way makes hint of divine nature or God's son any more than it makes Adam, who was born without the agency of parents, divine. Jesus was a human being who was created in a special and unique manner by God, Who is able to create what He wills as and how He pleases. The notion of the divinity or sonship of Jesus, the Quran asserts, is completely contrary to the true message which Jesus (peace be on him) brought of the Oneness and Uniqueness of God, and his insistence that God alone not himself was to be worshiped and obeyed (this topic will be discussed in greater detail later).

Muhammad (may God's peace and blessings be on him) was born nearly six hundred years after Jesus (570-632 AD) in Mecca, Arabia. He lived at a time when his people were in the grip of the worst form of idolatry and their society was in a state of marked corruption and decay. Within Arabia, Jews had formed tribes and settlements, but they did not propagate the message of the Oneness of God and the human being's responsibility to Him outside their own community. Christianity was splintered into many diverse feuding sects and its stronghold, the Eastern Roman Empire (Byzantium), was in a state of decline.

When, in the midst of this decadent society, a Messenger arose in the city of Mecca with the earnest, burning call to repentance and reform. He issued to the leaders of paganism a challenge which they could not afford to ignore if they were to retain their grip on the people. "*Arise and warn*" was the message with which God charged him. But his warning was met with the most intense hostility. At first he was ridiculed and opposed. Then with his small group of followers progressively exposed to abuse, defamation, torture, boycott and ultimately the threat of assassination. Every means the pagans could devise to induce him to give up his mission and force the early Muslims to abandon Islam was attempted. All of the early Muslims remained firm and constant, however, for their certainty of the truth of the Message was so strong that the mere threat of physical harm or death could not deter them from believing in it, proclaiming it and living it. Some of the first Muslims died under torture, and others migrated to Abyssinia to escape persecution, a country under the rule of a devout Christian king who subsequently secretly embraced Islam.

At length, after thirteen years of patient preaching and bearing with constancy all these trials, God opened to the Prophet and his followers the possibility of migration to the city of Yathrib (Medina) some three hundred miles distant, at the invitation of its inhabitants who had embraced Islam. They pledged their loyalty to the Prophet and swore to live and if necessary to die for Islam. The Muslims left Mecca in small groups and made their way across the desert to the city which had opened its heart to the new faith. When they had all gone, the Prophet put his cousin, Ali ibn Abi Talib, in his bed to fool the pagans (thinking that the Prophet was still in his bed) while together with his closest friend, Abu

Bakr, the Prophet left Mecca, by God's guidance, avoiding the pagans' attempts to assassinate him in Mecca and hunt him down on his journey.

In Medina, away from the continuous day-to-day persecutions of the pagan Meccans, the Prophet was able to give form and continuity to the community and system he had been commanded to establish.

Here the parts of the Quran constituting legislation concerning various matters were revealed, and here they were put into practice by the Muslims as soon as the verses were received by the Prophet. Here too the Islamic community and state, with all the various elements of social, political and economic life cast into a form which would be an example for all the future generations of Muslims, came into existence.

But even here there was no peace for the Prophet and his community. They were repeatedly harassed by the continued threats and military expeditions of the pagans, and by the opposition and treachery of dissident groups in and around Medina. Yet the Muslim community, although initially small in number and poorly-equipped for battle, resisted with such valor that after some nine years it was able to subdue these enemies by a series of actions, both military and diplomatic. The Prophet (peace be on him) then entered the city of Mecca—from which he had fled several years earlier under the threat of death—as the leader and ruler of a humbled populace. Instead of reproaching or taking any sort of vengeance upon those who had persecuted him so cruelly, he freely forgave even his most bitter enemies, and thus the "conquest" of Mecca took place without bloodshed. The Prophet entered the Kabah, the sacred house of God's worship built in antiquity by the prophets Abraham and Ishmael, and with his own hands broke into pieces the three-hundred-and-sixty idols which had been erected and worshiped there, purifying the Kabah once again for the worship of God, the Praised and Exalted, alone.

Prophet Muhammad (God's peace and blessings be on him) died a few years later. Truly he had delivered the message with which he had been entrusted by God, and he left behind for all time to come two permanent, unchangeable sources of guidance: the Holy Quran and his *sunnah*—that is, his own example and practice, the details of which were within some years collected in many well-documented verbal reports known as *Hadith* which have been presented accurately to the present time as the second source of guidance in Islam after the Quran.

After the Prophet, four of his closest friends and Companions—Abu Bakr, Umar, Uthman and Ali—became the leaders and heads of the Muslim society and state with the title *Khalifat rasool* Allah, that is, caliph or successor to the Messenger of God. They ruled scrupulously according to the guidance of the Quran and the Prophet's example. After them, however, the political leadership took the form of a hereditary monarchy which deviated markedly from the example of the Prophet and the first four rightly-guided caliphs. At the same time, Islam spread with great rapidity, carried to many parts of the globe by the Muslims whose individual lives and societies had been transformed by their faith. At its zenith (700 to 1600 AD) the Islamic Empire stretched from Spain to the Philippines, and, at a time when Europe was still in a very primitive state, the light of faith, learning and culture which illuminated Muslim lands was truly the beacon of piety and civilization in an otherwise darkened world.

The Quran is emphatic in proclaiming that Muhammad (peace be on him) is the last messenger of God, the "Seal of the Prophets," and that any who claim prophethood after him are false. But why, it may be asked, if God had sent messengers to earlier peoples as the need arose, and as the human being's course on this planet is not yet run and the need for guidance is so evident today should there be no further prophets after him? This is so because the Quran is God's final and complete guidance for all humankind. As such it does not require any amendment, abrogation or restatement. Moreover, it was revealed at a time when the human being's intellect, consciousness and the ability to preserve and transmit knowledge through writing had reached full maturity. The Quran has been preserved, word for word, letter for letter, exactly as it was revealed, and as long as it remains so (and the Quran contains Almighty God's promise to safeguard it from alteration until the last day), there is no need for any further revealed guidance. The Quran is complete and perfect, and its principles and teachings are as valid and binding today as at the time when they were revealed; for although the style and mode of human life have changed, the Ultimate Realities, the nature of good and evil, and the human being's own nature are unalterable and permanent verities which are in no way affected by the passing of time or changes in the human condition.

Besides this there is another reason why no further messengers are needed. Supplementing the guidance set forth in the Quran is the example of the Messenger, Muhammad (peace be on him). A divinely-revealed Book might contain God's guidance, but a Book was not enough; someone was needed to translate that guidance into action, to live it. And that someone was not to be an angel or a super-human being but a man like other men, a man from among the community to which the guidance was immediately addressed, who would serve as a living example to others and would give concrete form to the laws which God had revealed amidst the varied conditions of ordinary human existence.

Concerning the life of the Prophet (peace be on him), such a complete and detailed account has been preserved as has probably not been kept concerning any other individual in human history. Because of the absolutely unique position he occupied as the recipient of revelations from God, the Praised and Exalted, every act and detail of his life was of the greatest interest to those around him. Hence the narrations preserved in the books of *Hadith* (life and sayings of the Prophet) deal with all facets of his life, from the most personal matters to the conduct of war and the affairs of state. Consequently Muslims have before them in every aspect of their lives—and it is to be borne in mind that in the Islamic frame of reference no part of the human being's existence is outside the pale of religion—the living example of the best of human beings. As his wife Aisha said concerning him that his conduct was the Quran. And while Muhammad (peace be on him) was an individual of immense spirituality and nearness to God, at the same time he also lived an extremely full, active and complete life, exemplifying many varied and complex roles. He was a devoted husband, father and grandfather, a kind and responsible kinsman, a faithful, affectionate friend, a leader alike in worship and battle, a ruler and statesman par excellence. For the Muslims of his time as well as for the Muslims of today and tomorrow, he was, is and will always be the model: the teacher, the guide, the leader, and above all the conveyor of the divine guidance, the connecting link with God, and the person whom they love, revere and emulate above all other men.

> *"You have indeed in the Messenger of God a beautiful pattern for any whose hope is in God and the Last Day, and who engages much in the praise of God."* (33:21)

> *"O Prophet, truly We have sent you as a witness, a bearer of glad tidings and a warner, and as one who invites to God by His leave, and as a lamp spreading light. Then give the glad tidings to the believers that they shall have from God a very great bounty."* (33:45-47)

Now there have been many claimants to prophethood, some even in modern times. How, therefore, can anyone prove that Muhammad's claim to be a messenger of God, to have received divine revelation, is true? In short, could Muhammad actually and in fact have been the Messenger of God, the Last Prophet, or did he merely imagine he was or pretend to be?[9]

The real question being asked is in fact: How can one distinguish a true prophet from a false one? In order to determine the truth of any person's claim to have brought a divinely-revealed scripture, it is necessary to establish some rigorous criteria which are generally acceptable in terms of logic and reason. These criteria should be such that in the light of them anyone may searchingly examine any scripture, whether it is the Quran, the Old and New Testaments, the Bhagava-Gita or any other religious text, and decide for himself whether or not it deserves serious consideration as coming from the Lord of the universe. Such criteria may be something like the following:

* The person claiming to have received revelation should be known as an individual of unblemished character and morals, of whom no evil or sin is known. In particular, he must be of the strictest standard of honesty and truthfulness.

* The words of the alleged scripture should be recorded exactly as they were received from the divine Source, without the slightest interference or change on the part of anyone, including the one who claimed to have received the revelation. The original scripture should remain intact and accessible to anyone who wishes to read it.

* The message contained in the scripture should be totally consistent throughout. No part of it should contradict any other part.

* There should be no confusion among its concepts and teachings.

* Nothing in it should be contrary to the objectivity observed facts of the natural world.

* It should appeal to human reason and rational faculties rather than to irrationality, superstition and the like.

* It should provide spiritual insight and moral guidance of the highest order.

* It should not attribute to God anything which is contrary to His unique, exalted and transcendent nature, nor to any created being anything which pertains exclusively to God.

* It should emphatically deny to anyone other than God the right to be worshiped and obeyed.

* It should emphasize brotherhood and equality among human beings, and should not uphold the domination of some people by others.

* It should not attribute major sins and vices to the persons whom God singled out for the task of conveying His guidance (the prophets), for this is tantamount to attributing lack of knowledge or stupidity to God.

* Its language should be eloquent and sublime and of the highest order of literary style and expression.
* Although it is not essential as a proof of its truth, if it contains objectively verifiable information such as could not be known by anyone other than the Creator, it will be considered a further testimony to its truth and genuineness.

If the reader should be interested in carrying out such an examination of the Quran, it is important that he approach it with a completely open mind, uncolored by earlier preconceptions or prejudgments about Islam and its Book. It is also suggested that he begin his reading of the Quran from the far end rather than from the beginning, or, if he plans to read bits and pieces rather than the whole of it, to open it anywhere he pleases at any point in his reading. The reason for this is that the Quran is not a volume with the sequential order of a conventional book and thus it may be opened and approached from any portion or page. The most powerful and moving *surah*s (chapters) are by and large found in the latter portion of the Book, while the long *surah*s near the beginning contain considerable matter dealing with legislation, the early Muslim community, relations with non-Muslims, the histories of earlier prophets and their peoples, and various other subjects. It is also suggested to use a translation by a Muslim rather than by a non-Muslim, as it is likely to be more accurate and true to the spirit of the Arabic,[10] and, if possible, one containing a commentary for clearer understanding.

From such an examination of the Quran, we can make the following important points:

* We observe that Muhammad brought a Message over a period of twenty-three years which, from the first revelation to the last, was totally consistent with itself, without any contradiction, confusion or change.
* The wording of the existing Quranic text (of which there is only one standard Arabic version throughout the world) remains word-for-word exactly as Muhammad received

it. Its verses and sections are in the exact order in which he himself placed them as commanded by divine revelation.

* We observe that the language of the Quran is completely different from the speech of Muhammad which has been recorded in his exact words in the voluminous collections of *Hadith*, and that it has a unique, sublime, exalted quality which is also different from the speech of any human being before or since which even the enemies of the Prophet, despite their most strenuous efforts, were unable to imitate.

* The concept of God and of the Ultimate Realities which the Quran expresses is of the utmost degree of fitness and sublimity as are the spiritual truths and moral guidance it sets forth.

* Muhammad did not know how to read or write, nor was he learned in any branch of knowledge. Although he may have had some idea about the basic teachings of Christianity and Judaism, his knowledge of these religions cannot have been more than quite superficial. However, the Quran contains innumerable references to these religions, their teachings and the histories of the earlier prophets in such depth and detail as could not possibly have been mastered by anyone who was not literate and of a very high degree of religious knowledge. In addition, other elements of the Message he brought are such that it would have been impossible under any circumstances for an illiterate Arab of his time either to master or to construct them within his own mind impossible, indeed, for any human being of any time or place, for a great part of them relate to *al-ghaib*, the Unseen Realities, containing information which can be known only to the Creator of all things.

* Not only does the Quran contain nothing which is contrary to reason or objectively observed facts, but it repeatedly appeals to the human being to use his reason and logical faculties to verify the truth of its message. In particular,

it cites example after example from the natural world as a proof of God's limitless power and wisdom. In addition to this, it also contains matter related to the world of nature which was not known or understood by anyone until many centuries later. Here are only three examples:

"Do those who disbelieve not see that the heavens and the earth were of one piece, then We parted them? And We made every living thing of water. Will they not then believe? And We placed in the earth firm hills lest it quake with them and We placed therein ravines as roads that they may find the way. And We have made the sky a roof withheld (from them), yet they turn away from its signs. And it is He Who created the night and the day, and the sun and the moon. They float, each in an orbit." (21:30-33)

"And God created every animal from water. Among them is that which goes upon its belly and among them is that which goes on two legs and among them is that which goes upon four. God creates what He wills. Verily, God has power over all things." (24:45)

"Verily, We created the human being from a quintessence of wet clay, then placed him as a drop in a safe lodging. Then We made the drop a clot. Then We made the clot a lump, then We made the lump bones, then clothed the bones with flesh, and then produced it as another creation. So blessed be God, the best of creators." (23:12-14)

These verses, which first came to light in sixth century Arabia, are so extraordinary that it is worthwhile to study them very closely. Was there anyone in Muhammad's area who had the remotest inkling of the processes be which the universe came into being, or that all life, and every form of animal, originated from water, or of the balancing force which mountains provide to the earth, or the fact that the heavenly bodies all "float" along "in orbit?" For views less heretical than these the scientists of

Europe were called to account by the Inquisition centuries later. Or was there anyone during his time who understood the detailed stages and processes be which a drop of sperm becomes a human infant? And these are not unique examples. The Quran is full of statements concerning the natural world which totally conform to modern scientific findings, some of which could not have been understood in scientific terms by anyone until fairly recent times.[11] Moreover, the Quran exhibits an extraordinary depth of insight into human nature, particularly in relation to the contrasting states of mind of one who is deeply grounded in faith in God and one who is in a state is disbelief or rebellion against Him. In this it outshines the most subtle contemporary researches into human psychology, dwelling on the state of peace, balance, direction and contentment of the believer on the one hand, and the inner emptiness, anxiety, depression and confusion of the nonbeliever on the other.

   * Finally, we note that the man who brought this scripture was renowned among his people for his faithfulness, good character and honesty. He was so respected for his truthfulness and upright character that his fellow Meccans had honored him with the title of *"al-Ameen"* (the Trustworthy) years before the beginning of his call to prophethood. He repeatedly warned others with the utmost urgency of the enormity of attributing anything to God, Whose displeasure he feared more than anyone because of the immensity of the responsibility which had been laid upon him. Could such a man. then, have been the forger, over a period of more than two decades, of a scripture which he claimed was revealed to him by God but which was actually of his own fabrication?

   In view of all the foregoing, one is left with only two possible explanations of the scripture called the Quran: either that Muhammad really was what he claimed to be, the individual to whom God Most High had entrusted the awesome task of conveying His ultimate guidance to mankind, or that he was the most outrageous and flagrant liar and deceiver who ever lived; and this is so totally at variance with everything that is known about him as to be absolutely impossible. But even if we accept for a moment for the sake of argument the possibility that Muhammad made up the entire Quran over this long period of time, we are still left without any explanation of how even the most audacious forger could have had knowledge of the many matters in the Quran which it is absolutely impossible that any human being of his time could have known or even remotely imagined, how the whole Quran could be so utterly consistent and free of contradiction, of such sublime depth and inimitable language, and how it could have such a convincing. unassailable, earnest ring of truth in its exposition of the Ultimate Realities.

Some have tried to explain away the Quran by alleging that Muhammad was mad or epileptic. But has there ever been, in all of human history, an instance of a person in the grip of epileptic seizures, insanity or any other form of mental aberration producing anything so consistent and coherent, of such profound depth and wisdom, something which was beyond the knowledge of any human being and which was beyond the capacity of the sanest and wisest men to produce?[12]

The pagan Meccans of Muhammad's own time, trying their utmost to avoid coming to grips with the truth of what he brought, tried in vain to explain away his message by similar allegations, and by claiming that he must be in the grip of poetic frenzy, or a soothsayer or one possessed; they even suggested that someone learned in Christian doctrines must be teaching him. But Muhammad had no knowledge at all of composing poetry, nor did he have any of the well-known bizarre characteristics of a soothsayer or a man who is possessed. As for the "teacher" theory, it could not be carried very far with a person who was always in full view of his enemies as well as of his followers (who both, for their own individual reasons, scrutinized with utmost care every detail of his life), and who often received the divine revelations in their presence.

Hence these charges were soon dropped, and even his most implacable enemies were forced to come to the conclusion that what he was receiving was indeed, as he claimed, from God. Moreover, he asked nothing for himself. No one can debate the fact that he had nothing whatsoever to gain and everything to lose—his life itself—by persisting in his mission in the face of the relentless persecutions of the pagans; while if his aim had been to achieve fame, power or wealth (the only possible motivations which can be ascribed to him if his message was not what he claimed), the pagan Meccans did in fact offer him all these and would gladly have given them to him instantly to deter him from proclaiming his revolutionary statement of the human being's accountability to God and the brotherhood and equality of all Muslims which threatened to destroy the entire edifice of their power, prestige and decadent life-style.

Consequently if we return to the message and look at the sublime concepts and ideas it embodies: its total consistency from beginning to end; the lofty standard of morality and human interaction it lays down; its profound, self-evident wisdom and depth; the extremely noble, earnest, moving quality of its tone and language: and what it contains relating to matters not then known to any human being on earth (least of all to an illiterate Arab) concerning the physical universe as well as the Unseen Realities; it becomes impossible to ascribe the Quran to human authorship. As a result, having ruled out every other possible explanation for the phenomenon of the Quran, we are compelled to conclude that it is, as Muhammad (peace be on him) proclaimed, the word of Almighty God. In the words of the Quran itself:

> *"So I swear by all that you see and all that you do not see that this verily the speech of an honored messenger (Gabriel). It is not the speech of a poet; little is it that you believe. Nor is it the speech of a soothsayer; little is it that you remember, (This is) a revelation from the Lord of the worlds. And if he were to invent any sayings concerning Us, We would assuredly seize him by his right hand and cut off his life-artery, and not one of you could keep Us from him. And verily, this is a reminder for the God-conscious. And We surely know that some among you will deny it, and that it is indeed a source of sorrow to the unbelievers. But verily it is the truth of assured*

certainty. So glorify the name of your Lord, the Almighty."
(69:38-52)

> *"And thus have We, by Our command, sent inspiration to you. You did not know (before) what revelation was and what faith was, but We have made it (the Quran) a light with which We guide such of Our servants as We will, and verily you guide to the straight way—the way of God, to Whom belongs whatever is in the heavens and whatever is on earth. Behold (how) all affairs tend towards God."* (42:52-53)

> *"This Quran is not such as can be produced by anyone other than God. It is a confirmation of earlier revelations and a detailed explanation of the Scripture (the totality of divine guidance since the beginning of human history on earth) in which there is no doubt from the Lord of the worlds."* (10:37)

Then what about the claims made by other "prophets," of either ancient or modern times that they too received revelations from God and perhaps a scripture? Again, we must go to the messages they brought and examine them carefully in the light of stringent criteria such as those suggested earlier for determining the truth of a scripture. Next we carefully examine the lives of the "messengers" themselves to see whether they conform to any sort of an accepted standard of righteousness and purity intelligence and credibility.[13] Then if the claimants to prophethood of either ancient or modern times do not meet such criteria as we may consider to be an objective and valid test of truthfulness and credibility, we are forced to regard their claims as fabrications and those who brought them as deliberate forgers and deceivers of their fellow human beings. In many passages the Quran speaks of the terrible punishment which will come to those who invent lies against God, as in the following:

> *"And who does more wrong than one who fabricates lies concerning God or who says, 'I receive revelations,' when he does not receive revelations at all, or who says, 'I will reveal the like of what God has revealed?' And if you could see when*

*the wrong-doers are in the pangs of death and the angels
stretch out their hands, (saying), 'Render up your souls. This
day are you recompensed with the punishment of degradation
because of what you spoke about God without truth and
because you scorned His signs.'"* (6:93)

And it is up to every human being to use the intelligence God
gave him to determine the credibility of such claims for himself,
for truth and falsehood are two different things and each can be
recognized by its own special characteristics.

THE HEREAFTER

*"Verily We shall give life to the dead, and We record all
that they send before and that they leave behind, and We have
taken account of all things in a clear Book (of evidence)."*
(36:12)

*"And to every soul will be paid in full (the fruit) of its
deeds, and He knows best all that they do."* (39:70)

Belief in the hereafter—what pertains to the day of judgment, bodily resurrection, and heaven and hell—is another basic
article of faith in Islam.

As we have already seen, Islam asserts that the present life is
but a minute part of the totality of existence. The Quran informs
the human being of the reality of another life of a very different
nature from the life of this world, of infinite duration. For God,
the All-Wise, All-Powerful Creator, is able to do anything He
pleases. He is easily able to transform His creations from one
state of being to another. Can we for a moment imagine that it
can be more difficult for Almighty God to raise us up when we
are dead than it was to create us in the first place? The Quran
speaks again and again of familiar and obvious examples of such
transformations: the coming to life again of the earth after it lies
dead and barren in the grip of winter or drought: the development
of a sperm and an ovum into an embryo in the environment of the
mother's womb, and its further development from that state into

a thinking, feeling, acting human being living in the world.

> *"And among His signs is this: You see the earth barren and desolate, but when We send down rain to it, it is stirred to life and yields increase. Verily, He Who gives life to the dead earth can surely give life to the dead. Lo! He has power over all things."* (41:39)

> *"O mankind! If you are in doubt concerning the resurrection, then, verily, We created you from dust, then from a drop, then from a clot, then from a lump of flesh (both) shaped and shapeless, that We may make it clear for you. And We cause what We will to remain in the wombs for an appointed time, and afterwards We bring you forth as infants: then you attain your full strength. And among you there is he who dies (young) and among you there is he who is brought back to the most abject time of life so that, after knowledge, he knows nothing. And you see the earth barren, but when We send down water on it, it thrills and swells and puts forth every lovely kind (of growth). That is because God is the Reality, and it is He Who gives life to the dead, and it is He Who has power over all things, and because the Hour (of Judgment) will come concerning which there is no doubt, and because God will raise those who are in the graves."* (22:5-7)

> *"Does not the human being see that it is We Who created him from sperm? Yet behold, he is an open adversary. And he makes comparisons for Us, and forgets his own creation. He says: 'Who can give life to bones wiser they are decomposed?' Say: 'He will give them life Who created them the first time, for He knows about every kind of creating.'"* (36:77-79)

> *"Then how can you reject faith in God, seeing that you were without life and He gave you life; then He will cause you to die and will bring you to life again, and again, to Him will you return."* (2:28)

As we have seen, Islam lays the greatest stress on the individual's accountability to God. The human being's life in this world constitutes a trial, an examination period, during which he prepares himself, either for good or for ill, for the next life of infinite duration. The day of judgment may be compared to the ending of the examination, during which the Teacher will ask each individual student, "What were you doing during the exam?" and will then evaluate the work he hands in. For although the human body dies, his soul, his personality has an existence extending beyond the present life: it is a continuous entity whose inner state will accompany it into the hereafter. It is this state, together with one's deeds, which will determine one's ultimate destiny.

It is obvious that an individual who has lived with the correct awareness of and relationship to Reality through submission to God Most High is in an entirely different inner state from one who has lived all his life with an incorrect or distorted awareness of Reality and in forgetfulness, rebellion and ingratitude vis-a-vis God, and who has died in this state. Moreover, although many of the deeds of such people may appear outwardly similar, they have been motivated by entirely different intentions: the one to obey and please God and the other for any reason other than pleasing God, Whose reality he does not acknowledge. Indeed, the differences between the inner states of such persons is so great that their being kept apart from one another, in entirely different environments corresponding to what is within them and among companions having a similar inner condition, is a requirement of the most rudimentary conception of justice, not to speak of the absolute, unswerving justice of the All-Knowing, All-Wise, Infinitely Just and at the same time Most Merciful God.

In very vivid, awe-inspiring language, the Quran sketches over and over the outline of the events of the last day. At a time when God sees fit, which is known only to Him, this world will be brought to an end in a terrifying cosmic cataclysm frightful beyond imagination. And on that awesome day of judgment, the bodies of the dead will be raised from their graves and rejoined with their souls, while those who were alive on earth at that time will die and be joined to this assembly. All people, past and present, will then stand before God, each one as totally alone and helpless as when he came into the world, to render their accounting:

> *"When the sky is rent asunder and attentive to its Lord in fear, and when the earth is flattened out and has cast forth all that was within it and become empty, and attentive to its Lord in fear, O human being! fierily you are ever laboring on laboriously toward your Lord, and you shall meet Him. Then he who is given his record in his right hand will surely receive an easy reckoning and will return to his people joyfully. But as for him who is given his record behind his back, he will invoke destruction and will be thrown to scorching fire. Verily, he lived among this people happily; truly he did not think that he would have to return (to us). Nay, but lo! his Lord was watchful of him. So I do swear by the ruddy glow of sunset, and by the night and what it envelopes, and by the moon when it is at the full, you shall surely travel from stage to stage."* (84:1-19)

> *"Then when there comes the deafening noise, that day a man shall flee from his brother and his mother and his father, and his wife and his children. Each one of them that day will have enough concern (of his own) to make him indifferent to the others. Some faces that day will be beaming, laughing, rejoicing. And other faces that day will be dust-stained: blackness will cover them. Those will be the deniers of God, the doers of iniquity."* (80:33-42)

Then those who denied God and rejected His guidance, who devoted themselves to the worship of deities other than God, and who did evil deeds will be consigned to a fearsome and terrible abode in which their companions will be others who, like themselves, are completely alienated from God. There they will be in a state of enduring torment and agony from which there will be no respite. They will long to have another chance to return to the world to live their lives differently in the light of their present knowledge of Reality, but it will be too late. The examination will be over and all the books closed. They will have no choice but to acknowledge the justice of their destiny which is due to what their own hands wrought, in spite of all the clear warnings which were sent to guide them.

> *"And on the day those who disbelieve will be placed before the fire, (they will be asked), 'Is not this real?' They will say, 'Yes, by Our Lord.' He will say, 'Then taste the punishment because you disbelieved.'"* (46:34)

> *"Verily, the sinners will be in the punishment of hell, to remain therein. It will not be lightened for them and they will be overwhelmed in despair. And We shall not be unjust to them, but it is they who have been unjust to themselves."* (43:74-76)

As for those who believed in God, who obeyed and submitted to Him and lived their lives for His pleasure, and who left this life in a state of surrender to Him, a state of unutterable contentment and satisfaction awaits:

> *"O My servants, no fear shall be on you that day nor shall you grieve those who have believed in Our signs and submitted. Enter the garden, you and your wives, in rejoicing."* (43:68-70)

> *"Those who believe and do righteous deeds, they are the best of creatures. Their reward is with their Lord: gardens of paradise beneath which rivers flow. They will dwell therein forever, God well-pleased with them and they with Him. This is for those who hold their Lord in awe."* (98:7-8)

These two states, heaven and hell, will be experienced in physical form by the new bodies with which God will raise people up: they are not merely spiritual or psychic states. And while we do not know their exact nature, the Quran tells us that the inhabitants of heaven will experience some things which will remind them of their life on earth, that the happiness and beauty of it will far exceed anything one can imagine, and that the ultimate triumph and bliss for those who have attained paradise will be in nearness to their Lord. As for those who have deserved hell, theirs will be a temporary or permanent state of torture depending on their inner condition and the nature and extent of their sins. The Quran describes hell as a state of intense, fearful burning and agony without respite, among the most horrifyingly loathsome surroundings and companions. But the most awful part of the suffering of its inhabitants will be the terrible. inescapable awareness that this is the destiny which they deserved and brought upon themselves by rejecting God and ignoring the guidance which He had conveyed to them through His messengers.

This clear reality of the future life is always before the mind and consciousness of the devout Muslim. It is this awareness which keeps the present life, in the midst of the most intense happiness and the deepest pain alike, in perspective: the perspective of a passing, temporary abode in which one has been placed as a test in order to qualify and prepare himself for his future home. This perspective is essential for the maintenance of mental balance and stability amidst the difficulties of life. Yet no Muslim, even the best among them, imagines that he is guaranteed paradise; on the contrary, the more conscientious and God-fearing one is, the more he is aware of his own shortcomings and weaknesses. Therefore, the Muslim, knowing that God alone controls life and death and that death may come to him at any time, tries to send on ahead for his future existence such deeds as will merit the pleasure of his Lord, so that he can look forward to it with hope for His mercy and grace.

> *"When the sky is cleft asunder, when the stars are dispersed, when the oceans burst forth and the graves are overturned, a soul will know what it has sent ahead and kept back. O human being, what has made you careless concerning your Lord, the Bountiful, He Who created you, then fashioned you and then proportioned you? In whatever form He wills, He casts you. Nay, but they deny the judgment. And verily, over*

*you are guardians (angels), generous ones, recording; they
know all you do. Verily, the righteous ones will be in bliss, and
verily, the wicked will be in the fire. They will enter therein on
the day of judgment and will not be able to keep away from it.
And what will convey to you what the day of judgment is?
Again, what will convey to you what the day of judgment is? A
day when no soul shall have any power whatsoever for (another) soul. The command that day will be (wholly) with God."*
(82:1-19)

*"The likeness of the life of this world is as the rain which
We send down from the sky. By its mingling arises the produce
of the earth from which people and animals eat. (It grows)
until, when the earth is clad with its ornaments and is decked
out, and its people deem that they are the masters of it, Our
command comes to it by night or by day, and We make it like
a clean-mown harvest as if it had not flourished yesterday.
Thus do We explain the signs (of God) for people who reflect.
And God calls to the abode of peace. He guides whom He
pleases to a straight path. To those who do right is a goodly
(reward) and more (than that). No darkness nor shame shall
cover their faces. These are the people of the garden; they will
abide therein. But those who have earned evil will have a
reward of like evil; darkness will cover them. No protector will
they have against gods as if their faces had been covered with
pieces from the depths of darkness. They are the people of the
fire; they will abide therein."* (10:24-27)

THE DIVINE DECREE

*"What God grants to people out of His mercy, no one can
withhold, and what He withholds no one can grant apart from
Him. And He is the Powerful the Wise."* (35:2)

*"No misfortune can befall on earth or in yourselves but is
recorded in a Book (of God's decrees) before God brings it into
existence."* (57:22)

The final article of faith in Islam is belief in God's decree.

This is known in Arabic as *qada wa qadar*, meaning the "mea-sure" of what is ordained by God and His "plan."

Since the entire scheme and plan of creation is under the direction and control of the Almighty Creator and Sustainer, everything that is or that happens in the universe, from the small-est to the greatest events, is governed by God's will, an integral part of His eternal plan. Nothing can take place without His ordaining it, nor is there such a thing as a random, chance event.

Perhaps the meaning of this can best be illustrated by an example. To many people the miraculous events which are reported in the Quran or the Bible, or the possibility of revelation from God to mankind may seem unimaginable, mere superstition or fables because, according to their understanding of Reality, "God does not intervene in human affairs;" the same sort of argu-ment is often used—and has been since the beginning of time to justify the human being's disbelief in the guidance brought by the prophets the afterlife, and so on. The Muslim, on the other hand, possesses the clear certainty that God is absolutely real and that He is continuously active in all of His creation including the world of people. All that exists or takes place, therefore, is the expression of His will, from the behavior of each atom of matter to the large-scale occurrences of human history to events of cos-mic proportions. And since all of it is His, determined by His per-mission and decree, nothing that happens can ever be understood as "intervention" or "supernatural," or as a random, chance event devoid of meaning and purpose, whether it happens in the world of nature or in the world of human beings. In human life, ease and suffering alike, and the events which produce them, equally have a purpose and meaning, and are equally a part of God's infi-nitely wise plan for His creation.

Such a belief gives the Muslim a tremendous degree of inner certainty, confidence and peace of heart especially in the face of afflictions, for he knows that since everything is under the con-trol of the All-Wise, Most-Merciful God, the circumstances of his life are likewise under His control and direction, and hence are not without a reason and a purpose. Moreover, he lives with the assurance that whatever is to come to any individual, including death, cannot fail to come at its appointed time nor is it to be withheld by any means, while conversely, nothing which God has not decreed for him can be brought about by any means whatsoever.

This inner certainty frees the Muslim from fear of anyone or anything other than Gods for he knows that no one has the slightest power either to injure or to benefit him without His leave. If God decrees some good for him, no one can keep it away, and at the same time. if He decrees some harm for one, no one has the power to avert it except Him. The Quran expresses this very succinctly:

> "Say: 'Who guards you in the night or in the day from the Merciful?'... Or do they have gods who can shield them from Us? They cannot help themselves nor can they be defended from Us." (21:42-43)

And the Prophet (peace by on him) said:

> "When you ask anything ask it from God, and if you seek help seek help in God. Know that if the people were to unite to do you some benefit they could benefit you only with what God had recorded for you, and that if they were to unite to do you some injury they could injure you only what God had recorded for you." (*hadith*)

For God alone is the source of benefit or harm, and turning to anyone or anything other than Him for protection and help when everything "other" is itself dependent on His will is not only utterly futile but wrongfully attributes to others powers which God alone possesses, thereby distorting the accurate perception of Reality. In any situation, Islam teaches the task of a human being is to make a sincere effort, to strive, to do his best-not, as is so often incorrectly stated, simply to sit back and let things take their course in blind resignation to some supposed "fate" or "destiny"; for a human being does not know and cannot know wherein his destiny lies, and until he has exhausted all possible means and what is inevitable occurs, he cannot be said to have encountered that destiny. But then whatever God decides, whatever comes to one after all his efforts have been made, should be received with patient and trusting acceptance of what He in His infinite wisdom has seen fit to send, and with the expectation that it may prove to be a source of good and of ulti-mate blessing in the broader perspective of the life-to-come.

Belief in the divine decree is thus a statement of belief in the meaningfulness and purposefulness of all that is, an essential part of the Muslim's sense of total trust, dependence and submission in relation to his Creator. On these basic beliefs, then, the Islamic faith rests: the Oneness of God (Allah); the scriptures revealed by Him for the guidance of mankind; God's messengers, the prophets; the angels, His emissaries and agents; the hereafter: the day of judgment, the resurrection and the states of heaven and hell; and God's all-wise, all-powerful decree.

> *"The Prophet believes in what has been revealed to him from his Lord and so do the believers. They all believe in God, His angels, His scriptures and His messengers, making no dis-tinction among His prophets. And they say, 'We hear and we obey. Grant us Your forgiveness, our Lord, and unto You is the (ultimate and final) journeying.'"* (2:285)

II.
ACTS OF WORSHIP

Central to the Islamic teachings and way of life are various obligatory acts of worship (*ibadat*) which are often referred to as the "Five Pillars of Islam." These consist of (1) the declaration of faith, "I bear witness that there is no deity except God and I bear witness that Muhammad is the Messenger of God;" (2) the prescribed prayers; (3) fasting during the month of Ramadan; (4) the poor-due; and (5) the pilgrimage to Mecca.

While the aim of each of these acts of worship is the remembrance and glorification of God Most High, it must be emphasized that God's majesty and glory do not depend in the slightest degree upon the praise or even acknowledgment of His creatures, for He is absolutely independent of His creation and free of all needs. Rather it is the human being who needs these recurrent forms of worship to keep his contact with his Lord and his vision of the true Reality clear and strong. The purpose of Islamic acts of worship or practices is, therefore, to strengthen the individual's faith and sense of submission to God, to solidify his character, to discipline him for his role as God's faithful servant and steward on earth, to make it possible and easy for him to live in the manner ordained by God, and to reinforce the ties of brotherhood and affection among Muslims.

As will be seen in the following sections, these acts of worship require the participation of all aspects of human nature—his soul, his mind, his feelings and his body with its various needs and appetites, and his time, energies and possessions as well—and thus they are the worship by the total human individual of God Most High.

It will also be seen that the various forms of worship are prescribed at various time intervals. For example, the declaration of faith is to be always present in the mind and heart of the Muslim and to be uttered again and again with the tongue during his daily prescribed prayers. The daily prayers are to be performed five times every day of one's life after attaining puberty and even more often if one desires to strengthen his relationship with God further and grow nearer to Him. Fasting is for a full month every year, while the poor-due is to be calculated and paid once yearly, and the pilgrimage is to be performed once in a lifetime if possible (the latter two are obligations only on those Muslims who meet certain required conditions, as will be seen presently). These two aspects of the Islamic worship—the involvement in them of the total human being and the prescription of them at different recurring intervals—make them extremely unique and complete expressions of the human being's total dependence upon God and submission to His will, his utter humility and creatureliness before the greatness of the Creator, and his desire to serve and obey Him alone.

These acts of worship are obligatory upon all Muslims no matter where they may happen to live, whether they are part of a larger Muslim society or one happens to be a single Muslim living far away from any Muslim community. It is the collective obligation of Muslims to provide the means and facilities for carrying out these duties faithfully. Each of these acts of worship is prescribed in the Holy Quran, and each is performed in the manner in which the Prophet (peace be on him), who is the example for all Muslims of every time and place, himself performed them.

In this section we will discuss the concepts and significance of the various acts of worship. The details of how they are carried out have been left for a later section in the context of the daily life of Muslims, with the exception of the pilgrimage which, for the sake of coherence and continuity, has been presented in entirety in the present section.

1. DECLARATION OF FAITH (*SHAHADAH*)

" " Islam is based on five things: the testimony that there is
no deity except God and that Muhammad is His servant
and Messenger, the observance of prescribed prayer, the
fast during Ramadan, the payment of the poor-due, and the pilgrimage." (*hadith*)

The first of the acts of worship is to believe with the heart
and declare with the tongue that there is no deity except God and
that Muhammad is the Messenger of God. This is expressed in
the words "*Ashaduan la ilaha illa Llah wa ashaduanna
Muhammadan rasool* Allah" (I bear witness that there is no deity
except God and I bear witness that Muhammad is the Messenger
of God).[14]

Here, as we saw earlier, the word "deity" is used in the broad
sense which the Arabic word *Llah* conveys: that is, anyone or
anything who is worshiped, to whom one's love and devotion are
given and one's goal is directed: it also denotes that Being in
Whom is vested ultimate authority and the right to prescribe and
legislate, Whose words or commands are considered binding,
and Who alone is worthy to be obeyed. Thus it becomes clear
that this declaration has a far broader meaning than the words
convey in English. It is, in effect, a proclamation that the one
who believes and utters it cancels from his heart loyalty, devotion, obedience, submission to and worship of anything other
than God, the Praised and Exalted not merely of man-made idols
of wood or stone, but also of any conceptions, ideologies, ways
of life, desires, loves, preoccupations and authority figures which
claim his supreme devotion, loyalty, obedience and worship.

Similarly, "*Muhammadan rasool* Allah," although it is a very
brief, terse statement, denotes a whole train of thought beyond
the mere words as they are rendered into English. This proclamation of belief in Muhammad as God's Messenger is simultaneously a proclamation of belief in the guidance which that
Prophet (peace be on him) brought to mankind—God's final and
complete guidance for all humanity and at the same time implic-
itly a statement of the intention to faithfully follow that guidance.

2. PRAYER (*SALAH*)

" " *And be steadfast in prescribed prayer (salah) and regu-*
lar in poor-due (zakah), and whatever good you send
forth for your souls before you, you shall find it with
God. Verily, God sees all that you do." (2:110)

"*O you who believe seek help in patience and prescribed*
prayer. Verily, God is with those who patiently persevere."
(2:153)

"What stands between a human being and disbelief is the
abandonment of prescribed prayer." (*hadith*)

The second act of worship which Islam prescribes is the performance of prescribed prayers (*salah*) within certain established
time periods five times a day.

Why have prayers been prescribed for Muslims five times a
day? it may be asked. Would not once or twice, or whenever one
happens to feel like it, be sufficient? In answering these questions, it must first be pointed out that the Islamic prayers (*salah*)
are somewhat different from "prayer" as used in the Christian
sense, although personal supplication and glorification of God
(known as *du'a*) are also a very important part of the Muslim's
worship in addition to prescribed prayer. Actually, the word
"worship" in Arabic conveys the meaning of *salah* much more
accurately than "prayer"; accordingly we have retained the word
salah wherever possible in order to maintain this distinction.

Basically *salah* consists of recitations from the Holy Quran
and glorification of God accompanied by various bodily postures. The five times of worship correspond to the five periods of
the day: daybreak, noon, afternoon, the close of day, and night,
corresponding to the organization of the human being's time
around various activities. Keeping all this in mind, we can now
proceed to answer the above question of "why?"

Salah is a multi-faceted act of worship. Performing it regularly serves as a repeated reminder to the Muslim during the day
and night of his relationship with his Creator and his place in the

total scheme of Reality. Its purpose is to keep him from ever forgetting that he belongs, not to himself or even to the people who are closest to him, but to God, and that he is His servant, obedient to His command. The remembrance of Him and glorification of Him for a brief, concentrated period in the midst of his daily activities keeps this perspective always clear and intact. No matter how faithful or conscientious an individual may be, such reminders are essential, for a person's involvement in his human concerns and activities is so engrossing that it is very easy to lose sight of one's relationship with God, his place in the total scheme of things, his responsibilities, and his ultimate goal. The world around us is full of examples of persons who while they may be well-intentioned, have clearly forgotten who they are in relation to the total Reality and what their ultimate destiny will be.

This is achieved in part by the recitations from the Quran which are a part of every prescribed prayer.[15] These bring to mind not only the basic Islamic teachings concerning God, the human being, the universe and the hereafter, but they also recall the Muslim to his obligations to God, to other people and to himself, for as the Quran says,*"Salah restrains from shameful and unjust deeds."* (29:45) This continuous reminder keeps the conscience alive and functioning in a proper manner: without the reconditioning it undergoes by the regular performance of *salah*, it is likely to become estranged from its Source, inactive and easily corrupted. It will be obvious that prayer once a week or even once or twice a day simply does not fulfill this purpose and is moreover only a partial and very inadequate expression of the human creature's relationship with his Sustainer Who, in the words of the Quran, is *"nearer to him than his jugular vein."* (50:16)

In addition to this, through the bodily postures of the prescribed prayer, which consist of standing, bowing, prostrating and sitting, repeated a specified number of times in each prayer, the Muslim expresses submission, humility and adoration of God Most High with his entire being. The heart which is filled with the love of God, the consciousness of its own creatureliness and God's greatness and beneficence, indeed has an urge to express

all these feelings in physical as well as verbal form. By means of
salah, which enlists the participation of the human being's total
nature, Islam provides the means of expression in an extremely
dignified and moving form, for these needs and feelings.

Indeed, the self-discipline which is needed to perform *salah*
regularly and at the proper times—to perform the ablution which
precedes the prescribed prayer, and to carry on these prayers in
the early morning when sleep is so attractive, during the busy
daylight hours when one is preoccupied with work, family and
other activities, and at night when one is tired and wants to relax
or sleep—reaffirms the human being's total dependence on his
Creator and his position as His servant. *Salah* is truly the complete expression of the human being's voluntary submission to
Him. *Salah* is so important in maintaining this attitude of submission that it is obligatory even during any type of illness (certain modifications have been permitted to those who are ill, traveling or fighting in battle). And it is to be performed with strict
concentration, attention and presence of the heart, not simply as
a mechanical verbal and physical exercise. *Salah* and its significance to the devout Muslim are best described in the inimitable
language of the Quran:

> *"Verily, in the creation of the heavens and the earth, and
> the alternation of night and day there are signs for people of
> understanding—those who remember God standing and sit-
> ting and lying on their sides, and ponder over the creation of
> the heavens and the earth, (saying): 'Our Lord, You have not
> created this in vain. Glory be to You! Then save us from the
> punishment of the fire. Our Lord, indeed the one whom You
> admit to the fire You cover with shame, and for the wrong-
> doers there will be no helpers. Our Lord, we have heard the
> call of one calling us to faith: 'Believe in your Lord,' and we
> have believed. Our Lord, then forgive us our sins and blot out
> from us our iniquities, and take us to You among the righteous.
> Our Lord, grant us what You did promise us through Your mes-
> sengers, and do not shame us on the day of judgment; for
> indeed, You did not fail in Your promise.'"* (3:190-194)

A Muslim is required to pray at the prescribed times wherever he may be—whether in a mosque, in his home, at work, or in any other clean environment indoors or outside—but it is preferable and more meritorious to pray in congregation with his fellow Muslims if possible. In such a congregational prayer, in which Muslims stand in straight rows shoulder to shoulder as one body united in the worship of the One God, the elements of discipline, orderliness, brotherhood, equality and solidarity are very strongly exemplified. Non-Muslims who are seeing Muslims pray in congregation for the first time are often very much struck by this living expression of brotherhood, equality and discipline.

Because of all these aspects, *salah* is the principal means whereby the Muslim keeps his life in correct perspective, having always before his mind the limited, finite nature of this world's life, with all its allurements and involvements, pleasures and pains, and the certainty of death and the life-to-come, attempting to maintain a sense of balance and proportion between the needs and claims of this world and the hereafter. Through worship at regular, fixed intervals marking the periods and divisions of the day, the individual voluntarily affirms the relationship existing between himself, the servant, and his Master, God Most High, acknowledging and maintaining God's rights and claims on him in the midst of his involvement with his worldly affairs.

> *"God is the Light of the heavens and the earth. The similitude of His Light is as a niche wherein is a lamp. The lamp is in a glass; the glass is as it were a shining star, kindled from a blessed tree, an olive neither of the East nor of the West, whose oil is almost luminous although no fire has touched it. Light upon Light! God guides to His Light whom He wills, and God draws up parables for mankind for God is the Knower of all things. In the houses in which God is exalted and in which His name is remembered there are people who glorify Him at morning and evening—people whom neither merchandise nor trade takes away from the remembrance of God and constancy in salah and payment of zakah, who fear a day when the hearts and the sight still be overturned: that God may reward them*

*with the best for what they have done and increase the reward
for them out of His bounty, for God provides for those whom
He wills without measure." (24:35-38)*

3. FASTING (*SAWM*)

*" O you who believe, fasting is prescribed for you as it
was prescribed for those before you in order that you
may be conscious of God . . . Ramadan is the (month) in
which the Quran was revealed as a guide to mankind and as a
clear evidence for guidance and judgment (between right and
wrong). So whoever among you witnesses this month, let him
spend it in fasting; but if anyone is ill or on a journey, the prescribed period (should be made up) by days later. God intends
ease for you and He does not intend hardship and (He desires)
that you should complete the prescribed period, and that you
may glorify God for guiding you and that You may be thankful." (2:183, 185)*

Fasting is a practice common to many religions. Islam has
also prescribed fasting for Muslim in the form of a month-long
period of abstinence accompanied by intensive devotional activity which constitutes the third of the obligatory acts of worship.

Islam establishes a lunar calendar in which the months are all
either twenty-nine or thirty days long. The ninth month,
Ramadan, is the month in which the first revelation of the Quran
came to the Prophet (peace be on him). The fast of Ramadan has
been prescribed in order to train Muslims in self-discipline and
scrupulous obedience to God's commands. It is not related to
penance for sins or regarded as a means of appeasing God's
wrath as in some religions. Again, in distinction to the fasting of
some religions, the fast of Ramadan involves total abstinence
from all food, drink and sexual relations throughout the daylight
hours; not even water may be taken. However, the fast must be
broken at sunset each day, and it is also recommended to have a
pre-dawn meal before resuming the fast the next day.

In addition to refraining from meeting these ordinarily lawful necessities, Muslims also engage in increased devotional

activity throughout this month. Besides the usual five daily prayers, an additional *salah* called *taraweeh*, which is observed only during Ramadan, is performed either individually or in congregation each night. It is, moreover, a *sunnah* (practice) of the Prophet (peace be on him) to complete the recitation of the entire Quran during Ramadan and many present-day Muslims follow this tradition. The last ten days and nights of Ramadan are marked by especially intensive devotions, including the commemoration of the night during which the first revelation of the Quran came to the Prophet, known as the Night of Power. Giving charity is especially enjoined during Ramadan and restraining the tongue and temper are an additional aspect of fasting.

Fasting makes the Muslim disciplined, steadfast and resilient like a soldier who forgoes or postpones the satisfaction of his normal needs at the order of his Commander. This trains him to be flexible and adaptable in his habits, capable of enduring hardship, and not to take for granted the bounties of God which he normally enjoys. Fasting also enables the Muslim to feel with the poor who daily experience hunger and to be active in compassion and charity toward them.

Islam recognizes that physical needs and appetites, particularly those of food, drink and sex, are powerful factors in human life, tying the human being to dependence on and preoccupation with his bodily needs and desires. Hence the Muslim is asked for one month out of the year to do without the satisfaction of these needs by day in order to develop his spiritual nature. The process of experiencing hunger, thirst and sexual abstinence—of imposing them on oneself voluntarily, so to speak—has the effect of weaning a human being away from dependence on physical satisfactions and the dominance of his animal needs, freeing him to pursue spiritual goals and values during this period. Ramadan is thus a month, out of the twelve months of the year, during which the Muslim—due to the lack of his usual involvement with his physical needs—has a unique opportunity (which of course depends on his own initiative to utilize or forgo) to devote himself to God and to his spiritual development.

While such fasting may sound difficult to those who are not

used to it, in practice it is generally tolerable and even easy for most people. In fact, it appears to have some therapeutic and beneficial effects on the body which are not yet clearly understood in scientific terms. Indeed, Muslims often become so accustomed to the altered routine of Ramadan and experience such an intense spiritual life during it that when it ends they feel a poignant sense of loss and wait eagerly for the next Ramadan to attain the same high spiritual level again, carrying its experiences and lessons with them throughout the coming year.

At the conclusion of Ramadan, Muslims celebrate one of the two major festivals of Islam-the Festival of Ending the Fast (*eid al-fitr*). This occasion, as well as the practical details of fasting will be discussed under The Islamic Way of Life.

4. POOR-DUE (*ZAKAH*)

> *It is not righteousness that you turn your faces toward the East or the West but righteousness is that one believe in God and the last day and the angels and the Book and the prophets; and (that he) give his wealth out of love for Him for kinsmen, orphans, the needy, the traveler, those who ask, and to ransom captives; and (that he) establish salah and give zakah. And those who keep their commitments when then make them and are patient in tribulation and adversity and in the struggle: these are the truthful and the are the God-conscious."* (2:177)

The Arabic word *zakah*, which literally means "purification," has no actual and precise English equivalent; the term nearest to it in meaning is "poor-due." *Zakah*, the fourth of the acts of worship in Islam, is thus the Muslim's worship of God by means of his wealth through an obligatory form of giving to those in need.

Islam proclaims that the true Owner of everything is not the human being but God Who bestows wealth on people out of His beneficence as He sees fit. Hence those to whom He has given more have an obligation to spend from His bounty for their brothers or sisters who need help. In concrete terms, *zakah* consists of an amount which is assessed on the nonessential property of the Muslim, to be distributed among:

"The poor and the needy, and those who work on it (collecting zakah), and those whose hearts are to be reconciled,[16] and (to free) captives and (help) debtors, and in the cause of God, and for travelers." (9:60)

In addition to helping individuals who are in need or distress, *zakah* funds may also be spent (as mentioned above) *"in the cause of God,"* i.e., for the construction of mosques, religious schools and hospitals, and for the salaries of those involved in the propagation or study of Islam whose work keeps them from having time to earn a livelihood.

Zakah is not to be paid on property which is for personal use (for example clothing and household furniture, a house in which one lives a car one drives crops planted for domestic consumption) but is assessed at approximately two and a half percent per year on cash or capital which is beyond one's immediate needs as, for example, cash savings or investments, the inventory of a business, cattle, lands and crops which are a source of profit and so on. *Zakah* is to be paid once a year and is assessed on property only after a full year has passed since its acquisition and after any debts or other legitimate obligations have been met. Each Muslim's *zakah* is calculated individually, depending on the amount of *"zakah*-able" wealth or property he possesses and varying from year to year.

But why should this prescribed poor-due be called a "purification?" This is so because, since all wealth in fact belongs to God Who gives it in trust to people as He sees fit, a part of what one possesses is to be returned back to God in this form. The Quran speaks of the obligation of *zakah* in very moving words:

"Verily, the God-conscious will be in the midst of gardens and springs (in the next life), taking that which their Lord gives to them. Indeed, before that they were doers of good. They would sleep but little at night and in the early dawn then would pray for forgiveness and in their wealth (was remembered) the right of him who asked and him who was prevented (from asking, although needy)." (51:15-19)

Hence the payment of *zakah*, which is the share that God prescribed as the right of the Muslim community in an individual
Muslim's wealth. Giving it purifies his remaining possessions
and makes his ownership of them blessed. It also purifies his
heart from greed and selfishness and from regarding what God in
His bounty has bestowed on him as solely his by right. In turn
zakah purifies the heart of the one who receives it from envy and
hatred of others who are better-off. Rather than being his enemies
or exploiters, the affluent are his brothers-in-faith who acknowledge his right on what God has given them and, from His bounty, extend their help to him. The obligation of *zakah* has been
mentioned repeatedly in the Quran in the same sentence as the
obligation of *salah* to underscore its being a fundamental duty of
a Muslim, a prescribed act of worship. In fact, the first caliph of
Islam, Abu Bakr Siddiq, sent an armed force against a group of
people who refused to meet the obligation of *zakah* while observing *salah* and professing to be Muslim.

When practiced as prescribed, *zakah* is thus in effect a form
of social security in Muslim society. In prescribing this obligation, Almighty God assuredly did not intend to make people lazy
and expectant of receiving handouts. But in any society there will
always be people in distress and want for one reason or another
due to some calamity, war, a disabling condition, the inability to
find work, or orphans, widows and the aged who are unable to
work and who have no one to provide for them. Obviously there
must be some permanent, workable provision for these which is
also compatible with human dignity and which simultaneously
eliminates bitterness and envy between the rich and poor. *Zakah*
is thus an institutionalized, obligatory kind of sharing and caring
which equalizes the wealth in the community without, at the
same time, banning private ownership of property or stipulating
that all people must possess an equal amount of wealth, which is
contrary to human nature and to dynamism and development
within a society. It is to be remembered that *zakah* was instituted
fourteen hundred years ago. In spite of all the modern advances
in economic systems, methods of distribution of wealth, and con-

cern for the rights of human beings to have their basic needs met, no ideology or economic system has been able to develop any institution comparable to *zakah* for dealing with the problem of poverty while at the same time offering a solution to class rivalries and hatred.

Besides the payment of the obligatory *zakah*, Islam also urges Muslims to give voluntary charity, to the extent they can afford, to those in need. Indeed, charitableness is among the most stressed qualities in Islam. A Muslim is supposed to be always responsive to human need and distress and to regard his wealth as a trust from God which is to be used not only for himself and his family but for other human beings in need as well.

> *"You will not attain righteousness until you spent out of that which you love. And whatever you spend from (your) possessions, indeed God is aware of it."* (3:92)

> *"They ask you (Muhammad) what they should spend. Say: 'Whatever you spend that is good is for parents, the near of kin, orphans, the needy and the traveler, and whatever good you do, surely God knows it.' They ask you what they should spend. Say: 'What is beyond your needs.'"* (2:215, 219)

5. PILGRIMAGE (*HAJJ*)

> *And (remember) when We prepared for Abraham the site of the (Sacred) House, (saying): 'Do not ascribe anything as associate with Me, and sanctify My House for those who circumambulate it and those who stand and those who bow and those who prostrate themselves (there). And proclaim the hajj to people; they will come to you on foot and (mounted) on every kind of lean camel coming through deep ravines."* (22:26-27)

> *"The first house (of worship of God) appointed for people was that at Bakka,[17] full of blessings and of guidance for all kinds of beings. In it are signs manifest: the station of Abraham—whoever enters it attains sanctuary. Pilgrimage to*

*it is a duty people owe to God—those who can afford the jour-
ney. . . ."* (3:96-97)

Hajj—that is, pilgrimage to Mecca in Arabia—constitutes
the fifth and last of the acts of worship prescribed by Islam.
Obligatory once in a life-time for those Muslims who can afford
it—provided there is safety and security for travel and that provision is left behind for dependents—*hajj* constitutes a form of
worship with the totality of the Muslim's being: with his body,
mind and soul, with his time, possessions and the temporary sacrifice of all ordinary comforts, conveniences and tokens of status
and individuality which human beings normally enjoy, to assume
for a few days the condition of a pilgrim totally at God's service
and disposal, His servant who seeks only His pleasure.

Hajj takes place during the first days of the lunar month of
Dhul-Hijjah, with it's climax on the ninth of that month.[18] The
rites of *hajj* center on complete submission and devotion to God.
At the same time they commemorate as an example of such total
submission and obedience the Prophet Abraham, especially in his
willingness to sacrifice what he loved most in the world—his son
Ishmael—at God's command. (See Quran 37:99-113)[19]

People often wonder what Muslims do during their pilgrimage, what *hajj* is actually like. What follows is a brief description
of the principal rites and experiences of *hajj* and their meaning to
a Muslim.

Pilgrims come for *hajj* from all parts of the globe from the
Middle East, Southeast Asia, Africa, Europe, the Americas even
from Australia. The majority of them come by plane to Jeddah,
Arabia's major seaport which is about forty-five miles west of
Mecca. Others arrive in Jeddah by ship and still others travel by
bus or private car from neighboring countries such as Turkey,
Iraq, Iran, Jordan, Syria, Lebanon, Kuwait and other Persian Gulf
states as well as from various parts of Arabia itself.

As the pilgrims approach Mecca, at places designated by the
Prophet himself where pilgrim facilities have been constructed,
they enter into a state of consecration known as *ihram*. *Ihram*
signifies divesting oneself temporarily of all marks of status and

individuality to assume the humble dress and condition of a pilgrim devoted wholly to God. One takes on *ihram* by expressing his or her intention to enter into that state, making ablution or taking a shower, and putting on the pilgrim's dress (which is also called *ihram*). The dress of male pilgrims is a garment unique to *hajj*, consisting of two pieces of white, unsewn cloth which cover the lower and upper parts of the body. Although no specific garment is prescribed for women, they also enter *ihram*, wearing any garment which conceals the shape and covers them completely, leaving only their faces and hands exposed. Pilgrims in *ihram*, male or female, are to abstain from sexual relations, the use of perfume, quarreling, abusiveness and obscenity. They are also prohibited to harm any living thing, plant or animal (with the exception of dangerous insects, snakes, etc.) in the territory of Mecca, which, since the time of Prophet Abraham (peace be on him) has been designated as a sanctuary for all creatures. Pilgrims may, however, engage in all other lawful activities such as eating and drinking, sleeping, washing, commercial transactions, and so forth.

The pilgrim's first obligation when he arrives in Mecca after he has found his accommodation and taken care of his physical necessities, is to visit the Kabah and perform certain prescribed acts of worship following the example of the Prophet (peace by on him). Now just what is the Kabah?

Often referred to as the Sacred House (*al-bait al-haram*), the Kabah is a small rectangular stone structure[20] which stands inside the compound of the Sacred Mosque (*al-masjid al-haram*) in the center of the city of Mecca. The Kabah was originally built in antiquity by Prophet Abraham and his son Ishmael, also a prophet (peace be on them both), as the first sanctuary on earth dedicated to the worship of the One God. The story of the building of the Kabah is related in the Quran thus:

> "*And remember Abraham and Ishmael raised the foundations of the (Sacred) House, (saying): 'Our Lord, accept it from us, for You are the All-Hearing, the All-Knowing. Our Lord, make us those who submit to You and of our descendants*

a people who submit to You. And show us our rites, and forgive
us. Indeed, You are the Forgiving, the Compassionate.'"
(2:127-128)

And again,

> *"Remember We made the House a place of gathering for*
> *people, and of security. And you take the Station of Abraham[21]*
> *as a place for prayer. And We convenanted with Abraham and*
> *Ishmael that they should sanctify My House for those who cir-*
> *cumambulate it or use it as a retreat, or bow or prostrate*
> *themselves (there in worship)." (2:125)*

During the three thousand years since it was first built, the
Kabah was demolished several times by natural disasters or the
hands of men but each time it was rebuilt at the same site and for
the same purpose.[22] The celebrated Black Stone, thought to be a
meteorite, is known to be a part of the original structure: it is set
into one corner of the Kabah and, following the Prophet's example, the pilgrim kisses, touches or points to it while he makes his
circumambulations of the Kabah as a gesture of love and respect
for the significance of the Sacred House of God. The Kabah is
draped with a woven black covering embellished with Quranic
verses embroidered in gold. This covering is replaced annually
with a new one.

Because of its unique significance as the first house of worship of God, Islam prescribes that Muslims face the direction of
the Kabah whenever then perform *salah* this direction of the
Kabah from any place on earth is known as the qiblah.[23] Hence
millions of Muslims in every part of the globe turn their faces
toward the same central point five times a day as they offer their
worship to God. Since at all times some people in some parts of
the world are engaged in *salah*, the cycle of worship with its
focus toward the Sacred House continues uninterrupted. The
Kabah is the visible symbol of God's Unity, representing in concrete form His centrality in the life of the Muslim, the focal point
for Muslims of all times and places to turn toward in their wor-

ship as a symbol of their unity as one community submitting to the One God, a part of the endless stream of worshippers facing and circling around it unceasingly since remote antiquity in the glorification of God Most High.

For the Muslim, visiting the Kabah, whether it is for the first or for the tenth time, is a profound, awe-inspiring experience. The worshipper enters the Sacred Mosque by one of its doors with a supplication for God's peace and blessings. Looking beyond the throng of pilgrims and the patterns of columns and arches into the vast open courtyard around which the mosque is constructed, he catches a glimpse, with a tremor of awe and excitement, of the solitary black draped Kabah which is the center of every Muslim's world. After performing a brief *salah* of "greeting" of the mosque, he makes his way toward the Kabah through the vast array of Muslims of every place and race on earth[24] in order to perform the first of the pilgrim's rites, that of *tawaf* or circumambulation.

Seeking out the corner of the Kabah in which the Black Stone is embedded, from which the circumambulation is to start, with words of praise to God, the worshipper joins the host of Muslims circling the House and pouring out their hearts in supplication to Him. A sense of timelessness sweeps over him as he realizes that he is one atom in an endless ocean of those who have worshiped at this House since nearly the beginning of recorded history. Moving in that sea of worshippers within the shadow of the Kabah, a deep sense of his smallness and insignificance comes to him. All the trappings and defenses of his ego fall away as he realizes that God alone is great and that none of His slaves can bring any of his worldly props and privileges with him to confront the glory and majesty of his Lord. Here, under the blazing sun of Mecca, making his circuits around God's House as he repeats the solemn, moving supplications of the pilgrim, he comes face to face with his own nothingness, his creatureliness, his utter dependence on his Creator in the face of God's ineffable glory and sanctity grasping, in that brief yet intense encounter with the sublimity of God, that all the movements and efforts which people make on this earth are as nothing. They and he will pass away, and then he will come alone before the One who gave him his life to receive His judgment and the recompense for all he did.

After completing seven circuits of the Sacred House, the pilgrim may spend as much time as he wishes in making supplications to God in the immediate vicinity of the Kabah, and before he leaves he prays two cycles of *salah*. He will then probably go to the spring of Zamzam, situated underground within the compound of the Sacred Mosque very close to the Kabah,[25] to refresh himself with its water. He then goes to a nearby area within the compound of the Sacred Mosque to perform the next rite of *hajj*. This is known as *sa'i*, that is, "hastening" between the two small hillocks of Safa and Marwah, separated now by a long, marble-lined corridor, in commemoration of Hagar's hurried search for water at this site.

While the circumambulation of the Kabah centers around God Most High, the center of the drama of the hastening between Safa and Marwah is the human being. This hastening is symbolic of the human being's efforts and movements in this life, of the human soul's ceaseless striving in his journey through the world, together with the host of his fellow human beings. The worshipper walks and during part of the way may break into a run, seven times between the two lava-rock mounds, situated about a quarter of a mile apart, glorifying and supplicating God. Between the marble arches he catches glimpses of the adjacent courtyard of the Sacred Mosque.

At the center of it, like a luminous jewel, stands the black-draped Kabah around which, like an endless river flowing on and on day and night since remote antiquity, supplicants from every corner of the world, clad in the simple pilgrim's dress, move in utter absorption with God, uttering His praises and calling on His name. One who has visited the Sacred House leaves it with an intense longing to return to it again and again, and with a vivid understanding of why the Kabah is indeed the focal point of the earth for the worship of God, the Praised and Exalted, representing in concrete form His centrality in the life of the Muslim individual and community.

Pilgrims may arrive in Mecca to perform their circumambulation and hastening either immediately before the days of *hajj* or earlier, as they wish, in fact, thousands of pilgrims arrive in Mecca days or weeks before the immediate period of hajj in order to have more time to spend in devotion at the Sacred Mosque. However, the climax of the *hajj* occurs on the 9th day of Dhul-Hijjah, the day of Arafat.

Arafat is the name of a vast, empty plain some miles outside Mecca. It is treeless and barren, without any shelter from the blinding desert sun and encircled by stark, jagged purple-black lava peaks. It is to this plain that the entire assembly of pilgrims, numbering some two-and-a-half to three million people, moves during the morning of the 9th of Dhul-Hujjah in order to spend the afternoon up to sundown engaged in penitence and supplication to God. The pilgrims come by private car, by bus and on foot, in wave upon wave, an unbelievably vast gathering of human beings of amazing diversity, reciting in unison the fervent, moving pilgrim's call of response to his Lord. Thousands of tents have been erected on the plain for this occasion to shelter them.

After the noon and afternoon prescribed prayers have been performed together in the shortened form recommended for travelers and people have had a chance to eat and rest, the period of devotions begins. During the afternoon up to sundown, all these human beings, assembled here from every land and belonging to countless races and cultures, are completely absorbed in supplication to God Most High, glorifying Him, affirming their utter helplessness and dependence on Him, and yearning for His forgiveness and His pleasure, enduring all the fatigues and difficulties of travel and the pilgrimage itself, with its severe climate and hard conditions, for the sake of that intense, profound experience of pouring out their souls before their Lord. The vast, otherwise empty plain is filled with tents and with thousands upon thousands of pilgrims, tired and disheveled and totally humble before their Creator, standing with hands raised in supplication, many weeping in the intensity of their awe and devotion to Him. Some climb up the Mount of Mercy, a hill in the middle of the plain from where the Prophet (peace be on him) delivered his last *hajj* address to his people, to make their supplications. The gathering of Arafat brings vividly to mind the immense gathering of that awesome day when people's bodies will be brought out of their graves and rejoined with their souls and all will stand in utter humility before God Most High to await His judgment, a time when no soul will have anything to bring with it before God except its inner state and whatever little good it may have been able to do in this quickly passing life.

As soon as the sun sets, the exodus of the pilgrims from Arafat begins: they go as they came by bus, car or on foot in an endless stream which continues for many hours. Their next station is Muzdalifah, a barren, inhospitable, lava-rock wasteland a few miles closer to Mecca, where they perform the sunset and night prescribed prayers together, spending part of the night resting after the fatigue of the day and engaged in supplication to God. Here they also gather a number of pebbles to be used for stoning three stone columns representing satan which have stood since ancient times in the village of Mina. After their brief halt in Muzdalifah, all the pilgrims go to live for the next two-and-a-half or three days in a vast tent city before they complete their pilgrims' rites and disperse.

These stone pillars stand at the sites where satan appeared to Abraham and Ishmael (God's peace and blessings be on them) in remote antiquity, tempting them to disobey God when Abraham was taking his son to be sacrificed at God's command. On each of the three days of sojourn in Mina, countless numbers of pilgrims go to the columns, stoning the pebbles they have collected to symbolize their rejection of satan, in a stirring drama of the endless human struggle against evil promptings and temptations

After the first day's stoning (and after shaving or shortening of hair by men and after cutting a short piece of hair by women), the pilgrim may shower and return to his ordinary dress. Most of the prohibitions applying in the state of *ihram* are now lifted. At this time, following the Prophet's example and injunction, many of the pilgrims slaughter an animal in commemoration of Abraham's sacrifice of a sheep in the place of Ishmael. Part of the meat is used to feed themselves and their group, and the rest is distributed among the poor. During this period the pilgrims also return briefly to Mecca to perform their final circumambulation of the Kabah. The pilgrim's home during the days in Mina is a tent shared with other pilgrims of the same sex or with his family, within specified camp compounds provided by pilgrim guides or by various governments or organizations. He spends the time in making daily trips for the stoning, praying and reading the Quran, listening to talks about various aspects of Islam, visiting with his fellow pilgrims, or resting. Before sundown on the third day or the following morning he leaves Mina and his pilgrimage is now complete.

In addition to its unique spiritual aspects, *hajj* is also remarkable, as we have seen, for the fact that it brings together from every part of the earth such an immense diversity of human beings, who, in spite of vast differences of culture and language. form one community (*ummah*), all of them professing and living by the same faith and all devoted to the worship of their single Creator. One can see pilgrims from Turkey, from Indonesia, from India: Egyptians and Afghans, Tunisians and South Africans, Malaysians, Arabians, Iraqis, Sudanese, Libyans: old men with henna-dyed beards from Baluchistan or the frontier areas of Pakistan, Iranian women clad in chadors, men and women from the tropical areas of Africa with their distinctive dresses, and here and there such faces as can belong only to Europeans or Americans. It was this aspect of *hajj* which Malcolm-X commented on so eloquently in his *Autobiography*, describing it as a tremendously moving and almost unbelievable experience to be, for the first time in his life, regarded and respected simple as a human being who was the equal of every other human being without consideration of the usual man-made distinctions and barriers such as race, color, nationality or social status. This is assuredly the ultimate experience in human brotherhood known to human beings. And what is required of a pilgrim during *hajj* is not merely to be present, but to behave with kindness and consideration to one's fellow pilgrims (although in practice there are unfortunately many deviations from this requirement): indeed, one's entire pilgrimage can be rendered void by acts of harshness or hostility to others. As we have seen, *hajj* takes place each year during the specified period of pilgrimage. However, Muslims may visit the Kabah at any time to perform umrah, the "Lesser Pilgrimage."

The rites of *umrah* consist simply of the assumption of the sacred state, circumambulation around the Kabah, and hastening between Safa and Marwah. Outside the season of *hajj*, countless Muslims visit Mecca to perform *umrah* each year, and still others who live in Mecca or its vicinity visit the Sacred Mosque frequently for *salah*, meditation, reading the Quran, or to make *tawaf*, which in itself is a complete act of worship without performing *umrah* or entering into the state of *ihram*.

Although it is not in any way related to the observances of *hajj* or *umrah*, those pilgrims who are able, visit the city of Medina some three hundred miles north of Mecca during their trip to Arabia. There they visit the Prophet's mosque to perform prayers to God and visit the grave of the Prophet, which is situated within the mosque which bears his name, to ask God to bless and reward Prophet Muhammad for guiding us to God's only one and true religion. The Prophet's Mosque stands at the site of the small mosque where he prayed and preached, next to which he had his home. Visitors spend as much time as possible in the mosque engaged in *salah*, reading the Quran and meditation. It radiates an atmosphere of the deepest serenity and peace. As in Mecca, there are always visiting Muslims in Medina, and it possesses the same unique flavor of peoples from all parts of the world coming together for the worship of God Most High and here for the love and remembrance of His Holy Prophet (may God's peace and blessings be on him) as well.

PART TWO:
VALUES AND MORALS

III.
ISLAMIC VALUES AND QUALITIES

THE ISLAMIC PERSONALITY

" Verily, men and women who submit, and men and women who believe, and men and women who are patient, and men and women who are truthful, and men and women who are humble before God, and men and women who give in charity, and men and women who fast, and men and women who guard their chastity, and men and women who remember God much to them, God has promised forgiveness and a great reward." (33:35)

The goal of Islam of its concepts, acts of worship and teachings relating to values, attitudes, morals and behavior is to create an Islamic personality within the individual Muslim. Now just what is this "Islamic personality?"

Such a personality belongs to an individual who has rejected the supposition that there exists nothing but the material world, that the universe and one's own individual life, with all its circumstances and events, is the result of accident or blind chance, and who has accepted and lives by the certainty that there is a Being Who is responsible for all of creation and to Whom he, the human being, is in turn responsible. He acknowledges his dependence on this Being, accepts His laws as the rules which guide

73

his life, and surrenders himself to Him. He is always conscious of God, remembering Him in all his activities and concerns. Islamic values and attitudes are the base on which his personality is built and Islamic criteria govern all aspects of his life.

Such an individual, together with others like himself, forms an Islamic society which, collectively submits and conforms to the guidance of Almighty God. Islam proclaims that such God-conscious individuals, obedient to their Lord's commands, are the ones who will attain God's pleasure and His reward in the hereafter. A society composed of such individuals is therefore one which is capable of and suited to fulfilling the trust which God has bestowed on the human being of administering the earth and its affairs in a righteous and God-fearing manner. We will now take a look at the attitudes and qualities which Islam enjoins and which it fosters in the true Muslim—qualities which can be found, even in today's disturbed world, turned as it is away from spiritual values and toward materialism and the worship of self, in a striking manner in countless devout Muslims in all parts of the earth.

GOD-CONSCIOUSNESS (*TAQWA*)

"Verily, the Believers are those whose hearts feel fear when God is mentioned, and when His signs (or revelations) are recited to them they increase their faith, and who put their trust in their Lord." (8:2)

"Verily, those who live in awe for fear of their Lord, who believe in their Lord's signs (or revelations), who do not ascribe partners to their Lord, who give what they give in charity with their hearts full of fear because they are to return to their Lord: it is these who hasten in all good acts and they are foremost in them." (23:57-61)

The Arabic word *taqwa*, denoting a quality which is absolutely essential in the personality of the conscious Muslim, has no exact English equivalent. *Taqwa* refers to an attitude comprised of love and fear of God which we may translate, for want of a better word, as "God-consciousness." More exactly it refers to the constant awareness that one is always before God and that He knows everything concerning him, even his most secret thoughts. This attitude produces within one such an intense love for God that he wants to do only what is pleasing to Him; such great fear of God that he tries to avoid doing anything which He dislikes; and such a keen consciousness of God that he never for a single moment imagines His being unaware of what he does or that he will not be held accountable for all his intentions and actions. In the words of the Quran, the pious are:

> *"Those who fear their Lord in their most secret thoughts and who hold the Hour (of Judgment) in awe."* (21:49)

Taqwa is a vital attitude which develops little by little in the heart of the Muslim child as he is taught about the existence and omnipresence, the beneficence and kindness of God, his own total dependence upon Him, his Sustainer, and his personal responsibility and accountability to Him. Gradually there grows within him a constant awareness of the fact that he is always before God (As the Prophet said, "For if you do not see Him. He sees you,") a profound sense of personal responsibility, the habit of judging all matters by Islamic rather than by other criteria, and a love for God and for His way which guides all his actions. This is supplemented and enhanced by correct instruction in the principles and practices of Islam so that it becomes his total frame of reference; by an awareness of social, moral, political and other issues; and by the knowledge of the right and wrong of things so that he can fulfill his responsibilities to God, to other human beings and to society.

> *"The pious are those who spend (in God's way) in ease as well as in straitness, who restrain their anger and pardon people, for God loves those who do good; those who, when they commit an indecency or do injustice to their own souls, remember God and ask for forgiveness for their sins—and who can forgive sins except God?—and do not knowingly persist in*

*what they have done. For these the reward will be forgiveness
from their Lord and Gardens underneath which rivers flow, to
abide therein, and (God's) favor, the reward of those who
strive."* (3:134-146)

FAITH (*IMAN*)

*"To God belong all things in the heavens and on earth,
and God is sufficient as a protector."* (4:132)

*"Say: 'He is my Lord; there is no deity except Him. In
Him do I put my trust and to Him do I turn.'"* (13:30)

Islam makes a distinction between a person who submits to
God's guidance by obeying His laws (a *muslim*) and one who has
the deep inner certainty of faith (a *mu'min*: one who possesses
iman, faith, a believer), and indeed the difference is very significant. A *muslim* (submitter) may obey God's laws without real
depth of faith, while a believer both possesses this faith and acts
on it.

Now, faith to the believer is a great deal more than merely
"believing" that God "exists." Such faith is rather the realization
that this little piece of Reality which we are able to grasp with
our minds or senses is only a minute portion of the greater
Reality which is known only to its Creator. And it is the certainty that God is in absolute control of the universe, including the
human being and his world, and that, together with the rest of
God's creation, each one of us is wholly dependent upon God
and will return to Him for accounting.

But let us go back to the beginning, starting from the most
basic views of life in order to understand the meaning of such a
faith more clearly. There can be only two possible logically
acceptable ways to explain the universe and all that takes place
within it. Either it is, in totality, the result of randomness and
chance interactions, the correct but completely accidental collu-
sion of circumstances (which makes the earth nothing more than
the accidentally "correct" combination of particles of matter and
each newborn infant merely a fortuitously "right" organization of
chromosomes, cellular structures, nerve connections and bio-

chemical processes). In this case, the entire universe and all of human existence, including the events of each individual's life, can only be viewed as meaningless, purposeless accidentally interacting phenomena, the result of blind chance in the grip of which a human being is simply a helpless, hopeless, struggling victim making motions which may or may not be of use. In the grip of such nothingness, he himself is a nothing, and his life has not the slightest sense or purpose: he simply is because he happens to have been born and has not yet died.

Such an explanation, which can produce nothing within the human soul except a despair too profound to be borne, is not only totally at variance with all the observed facts of the universe, which speak in endless volume of a planning, willing power, creative beyond human comprehension, negating randomness in their eloquent testimony to the incredible organizational Will behind all that exists;[26] it is also totally unacceptable to the human mind, itself an incredibly organized, purposeful entity which seeks meaning in everything. One who uses his reason therefore has no choice except to realize that all that exists must be the result of the will, the plan and the decision of a Supreme Power. And since this is so, likewise every circumstance and event, either within the physical world or within the world of the human being, must also fit in with the will, the plan, the decree of this Power. In short, nothing which either is or which takes place is outside God's plan and will and occurs only with His permission and decree, including the actions of people since the human being too is a part of the scheme of God's creation and a part of His plan. We will return to this point a little later.

It is easy enough to understand the meaningfulness and purposefulness of things in relation to phenomena or events which exhibit some logic, order or sense, some may say. But how are we to understand it in the face of natural disasters, unexpected catastrophes and human tragedies which seem to do violence to logic, to order, to meaning, crushing and destroying all that is good in human life?

Again, we return to the two possibilities: that everything is the result of randomness and chance, or that it is the result, although why may not always be apparent to our finite, limited human understanding, of God's all-wise plan. If the former is correct and we are dealing with random and consequently mean-ingless events, then logically everything must be accidental and meaningless, for it is not possible that part of existence is the result of a planning Will and has meaning and purpose but some other part is accidental. Either all of it must be an accident, which it is impossible for the mind to accept, or all of it must be part of a plan and guided by the Planner. In either case the circumstances will of course be the same: whether we believe in the meaning-fulness and purposefulness of all that takes place or we believe it to be the result of blind chance, we may equally in both instances from time to time find ourselves in the grip of events which we are utterly powerless to control. But the difference between these two views is nothing less than the difference between confidence and despair, between serenity of heart and endless, crushing anx-iety, between living with trusting acceptance of what comes as being meaningful, purposeful and ultimately a source of good as it is the result of the will of the Merciful God, or with bitterness, anger, rebellion, and the intolerable weight of belief in nothing-ness.

At the same time, it is also clear that the human being has been endowed with freedom of choice and freedom to act. Does this not mean that he is, at least to some extent, independent and in charge of his own affairs? How does Islam resolve this very fundamental question of God's will in relation to the human being's freedom of choice and action?

To begin with, Islam places great emphasis on action, repeat-edly exhorting Muslims to strive, to make an effort, to do their best. Without action and effort nothing whatsoever can be attained or achieved. But at the same time, action and effort do not necessarily guarantee the results one desires.

Thus, for example, I make a decision, I choose a course of action, I act. To this extent I am free, within the range of choices available to me and depending on my capacity for action, which is obviously limited by my physical and mental condition and by the constraints of my environment. But what about the outcome of my decision, my choice, my action? Can I guarantee what it will be? No, I cannot. However, most of the time one's action does lead to the desired results.

For example, I decide to get up out of my chair and I am able to do it; I decide to go to work in my car and I go; I decide to get married, or to get a new job, or to invent a nuclear submarine or a Boeing 747 or to go to the moon, and I do all these things, dependent only on myself, on the cooperation of my fellow human beings, and on various machines and inventions. How then can one assert that I am not in control and that I do not determine the outcome of my actions? In short, where does God come into the picture?

Let us examine the matter in greater depth. It is obvious that to achieve the results I want I must will and act. I can hardly expect to get to work if I spend the morning lying in bed, to get a new job if I don't go out and look for one, or to get to the moon without the necessary efforts on my part to master the essential knowledge and skills. But even then my efforts do not guarantee the results I seek. All that may be said is that although the degree of effort has a direct relationship to the probability of achieving a desired outcome, nevertheless the outcome may turn out to be quite different than one intends. For example, I decide to get out of my chair as I've done thousands of times in the past but instead of doing it I collapse with a heart attack. I leave my house to go to work, having no doubt that I'll get there as I've done day after day for many years but I have an accident on the way and never arrive. I'm rich. famous and beloved but one day I learn that I have a fatal illness and in spite of all the medical skills money can provide I die in the prime of my youth and career. I am about to be launched in a spacecraft similar to others which have carried out their missions brilliantly but something goes wrong and it burns up in the take-off—one could go on and on enumerating examples.

In earlier times when life was simpler, few people entertained any question about the existence of God and His controlling will. They knew that their lives were dependent upon crops which were dependent upon such factors as rainfall and sunshine, which depended immediately upon what God willed. They knew, too, the limitations of their capacities to act, to shape their destinies, and these too were referred back to God's decision. But today, when our lives are run to such a large extent by the products of science and technology. It depends upon these as if they were gods themselves for the very control of our existence. We have totally lost sight of the fact that while we have been given the power—and indeed the obligation—to think, to plan, to choose and to act, we do not necessarily determine the outcome of our actions, which depends upon what God wills.

Nor do our existence, our faculties, our powers and capacities to act depend upon ourselves. Does any of us make ourselves so that we can determine our appearance or size or shape, our color or physical condition, our intellectual endowments and talents? And is there a single one of us who can by our own efforts control the beating of our hearts, the working of the cells and tissues in our bodies, the eventual process of disintegration and decline of old age, an accident or illness which overtakes us, or the death which is our inevitable destiny? If not, then the assertion that we are in control of our lives and are self-sufficient, which is the proud boast of contemporary Western civilization, is merely wishful thinking and self-delusion.

This notion of the human being's self-sufficiency has unfortunately led the Westerner to the conclusion that because he is able to do most of what he wills and undertakes, it is solely his willing and doing, aided by the invention and utilization of high-powered technological devices, which determines the results he achieves. Both the person and his intentions are presumed independent of anything except each other, and the fact that there must be Someone who gives the human being his nature and the capacity, power and means to carry out what he undertakes, and Who, at the same time, determines the results of his undertakings, has been totally lost sight of. Consequently, although many people still profess belief in Him, God, as the sustaining, planning, willing, acting Power in the universe, has been largely discounted in explaining the phenomena of "nature," as well as in relation to human affairs, and hence He has been "retired" from the lives of so many of us. In passage after passage, the Quran addresses itself to this point:

> "It is He Who created for you ears and eyes and hearts. Little do you give thanks! And it is He Who spread you in the earth, and unto Him will you be gathered. And it is He Who gives life and death, and His is the alternation of night and day. Do you then have no intelligence? Nay, but they say the like of what was said by earlier peoples.
>
> "They say: 'When we are dead and have become dust and bones, shall we then really be raised again? We were already promised this, we and our forefathers. Truly, this is nothing except tales of the ancients.'
>
> "Say: 'Unto Whom belongs the earth and whatsoever is in it, if you have knowledge.'
>
> "They will say: 'To God.'
>
> "Say: 'Will you not then remember?' Say: 'Who is Lord of the seven heavens and Lord of the exalted throne (of authority)?'
>
> "They will say: '(They belong) to God.'
>
> "Say: 'Will you not then be dutiful to Him?' Say: 'In whose hand is the dominion over all things, and He protects while there is no protection against Him, if you have knowledge?'
>
> "They will say: '(It belongs) to God.'
>
> "Say: 'Then how are you deluded?'" (23:78-89)

And again:

> "And among His signs is that He created you from dust, and then, behold, you are human beings scattered (far and wide). And among His signs is that He created for you mates from among yourselves, that you may dwell with them in tranquillity, and He has put love and mercy between your (hearts). Verily in that are signs for those who reflect. And among His signs is the creation of the heavens and the earth, and the variations of your languages and your colors. Verily in that are

signs for those who know. And among His signs is the sleep you take by night and by day, and your quest (for a livelihood) from His bounty. In that are signs for those who hearken. And among His signs He shows you the lightning in fear and hope, and He sends down rain from the sky and with it gives life to the earth after it is dead. Verily in that are signs for those who are wise. And among His signs is that the heavens and the earth stand by His command. Then when He calls you with a call, behold, from the earth you will come forth. To Him belongs every being in the heavens and the earth: all are obedient to Him. It is He Who begins creation, then repeats it, and this is easy for Him. To Him pertain the loftiest similitudes in the heavens and the earth, for He is the Exalted, the Wise." (30:20-27)

And yet again and again:

"All that is in the heavens and all that is in the earth glorifies God. Unto Him belongs the dominion and unto Him belongs the praise, and He has power over all things. It is He Who created you, yet one of you is a disbeliever and one of you is a believer, and God sees all that you do. He created the heavens and the earth in truth, and He shaped you and made you with good shapes, and unto Him is the journeying. He knows all that is in the heavens and the earth, and He knows all that you conceal and all that you reveal. And God is the Knower of what is in the hearts (of human beings)." (64:1-4)

"And with Him are the keys of the Unseen; none knows them but He. And He knows whatever is in the land and the sea. Not a leaf falls but He knows it, nor a seed grain grows in the darkness of the earth, nor anything fresh or dry but is (inscribed) in a clear Book. And it is He Who takes your souls by night and Who knows what you have done by day; then He revives you by day that a term appointed may be fulfilled. Then to Him will be your return, and then will He declare to you all that you did." (6:59-60)

> *"Say: 'Shall I take for my protector any other than God,*
> *the Maker of the heavens and the earth? And it is He that feed*
> *(His creatures) but is not fed . . . . If God touch you with afflic-*
> *tion, none can remove it but He; and if He touch you with*
> *goods (know that) He has power over everything. He is the*
> *Irresistible, (high) above His servants; and He is the Wise. the*
> *Informed.' . . . . Say: 'Do you think that if God's punishment*
> *were to come upon you, or the last hour, you would then call*
> *upon something other than God. (Answer) if you are among*
> *the truthful! Nay, you would call upon Him, and if He willed.*
> *He would remorse what occasioned your call upon Him and*
> *you would forget those whom you had set up as partners with*
> *Him'. . . . Say: 'Do you think that if God took away your hear-*
> *ing and your sight and set a seal upon your hearts, there is a*
> *deity besides God who could restore them to you?' . . . . Say:*
> *'Who is it that delivers you from perils in the darkness of the*
> *land or sea, upon Whom you call humbly and in secret: "If He*
> *only delivers us from this (affliction), we will be among the*
> *grateful?"' Say: 'It is God Who delivers you from these and*
> *from all (other) distresses, and yet you associate others with*
> *Him!'"* (6:14, 17-18, 40-41, 46, 63-64)

For indeed, when any of us is in a state of danger, terror or crisis, it is not other people or technology we call on; almost instinctively, as a matter of course, we call upon God, even if we otherwise never think of Him or even deny His existence. Anyone who has ever been in a battle or a wreck at sea or a devastating flood or earthquake or tornado (an "act of God"), or in the grip of a terrible illness or personal tragedy knows this and many have become believers as a result of such experiences. For at such a time each one of us recognizes the utter powerlessness of human beings and their inventions. We know unquestioningly that nothing can help or save us except the Supreme Power of the heavens and the earth, and quite unconsciously and without concern for our previous beliefs in the matter, we instinctively cry to Him for aid. And what about at the time of death? Is there a single one of us who then still entertains the illusion that the human being is in control and has anything to say about his own destiny, or who calls upon anyone or anything except God. For that is the supreme moment of truth, the truth which has always been there before our eyes but from which many of us turned away, as if deaf and blind, time and time again during the span of our lives.

In Islam we find the correct perspective concerning the human being's freedom of choice and action and the limits of his capacity to control events. For Islam informs us that every single thing in the universe, every atom of creation, is always dependent on God not only for its very being but for its continuance and functioning as well. In this human beings are no different from the rest of creation; despite the illusion that we are in control, our being is dependent on Him and we are sustained by Him at every moment of our lives, whether we are peacefully relaxing in the security and comfort of our homes or are in a state of critical danger or affliction.

This state of dependency, helplessness and creatureliness in relation to God is expressed in Arabic by the single concise word servanthood that is, the condition of being God's servant: one with whom God does as He pleases because he belongs to Him, who is totally at His disposal and in a state of utter dependence and humility before Him. To the devout Muslim, the highest honor and the fulfillment of his existence lies in being the *abd* [27] of God Most High, and of no one and nothing except Him. And part of the condition of this servanthood consists of the realization that the human being's task is to choose, to will, to act and to strive his utmost but that it is God Who determines the results of this striving as He sees fit. Therefore, beyond his capacity to act and to shape events by his action, the sincere believer trusts in and depends on God completely for the outcome of his affairs, assured that nothing that happens to him or to any other creature is a random, chance event, an "accident" or "coincidence," but has a meaning and a purpose which are known to God.

But we must be careful not to misunderstand this point, as many people have done and sooner or later lost their "faith" as a result. It certainly does not mean that if a person trusts in and depends on God in all his affairs, God will in return keep all trouble and suffering away from him; in other words, "If I'm good, God won't let anything bad happen to me." Indeed, this is not the way God has ordained this life, nor is this the attitude of a true believer. God sends both ease and suffering to all, the wicked and saintly alike, and certainly the sincere believer, like every other descendant of Adam, has his share of troubles, illnesses and calamities; in truth, he is more likely to pass through suffering and adversity as a result of his unswerving commitment to the right and his consequent lack of concern for personal comfort and worldly advantage. The difference is not in the circumstances but in the attitude: for the believer possesses the absolute certainty that God is in complete control of everything, knowing what the human being with his finite, limited human understanding cannot know, and since he believes that whatever God sees fit to send has a meaning and a purpose, he accepts it with the hope and assurance that it may hold some good for him either in this world or in the Hereafter.

For the whole of this life, both the good and the bad of it, constitutes a trial and a test for the human individual by means of which his quality and his state in the future existence are determined. Again and again the Quran speaks of this:

> *"Every soul must taste death; and We test you by evil and by good by way of trial. And unto Us will you return."* (21:35)

> *"Do people think that they will be left alone on saying, 'We believe and that they will not be tested.' And assuredly We tested those before them. Thus God knows those who are sincere and knows those who are pretenders."* (29:2-3)

But the test does not lie only in hardship and suffering. The rich, powerful and healthy individual is tested just as much by his wealth, rank and good physical condition as is the poor one by his poverty or the sick or handicapped by his affliction; indeed, the one to whom more has been given in the way of health or possessions or talents or status or power will be held accountable for more. What is of ultimate importance is not how much or little one possesses of all these benefits but what he does with whatever he has been given. For although a human being may not necessarily have a great deal to say concerning the conditions of his life or the outcome of a specific situation, nevertheless he is accountable both for his actions and for his inner response to the particular conditions in which he found himself.

The notion that a person's spirit and his deeds cannot rise above difficult or disadvantaged circumstances is one which Islam rejects, just as it rejects mechanistic views of any aspect of life. The human being is not a robot. Even in the worst of circumstances human beings have kept alive the spark of humanity and decency in their breasts and acted in ways which would do credit to the angels. Therefore, when faced with difficulties the sincere believer does all he can to deal with or to remove them, for he is not supposed to allow himself to be distressed or to bear suffering unnecessarily, and is expected to strive with all his strength to improve his situation. But if the desired results are not attained in spite of all his efforts, he does not despair nor does he dictate terms to God but rather tries to be patient and steadfast with what the Quran calls a *"beautiful patience"* (70:5). The Quran speaks in moving language of the way in which a sincere believer should bear trouble and affliction:

> *"And We shall undoubtedly test you with something of fear and hunger, some loss of wealth and lives and fruits. But give glad tidings to the patient, who say, when afflicted with calamity, 'To God we belong and to Him is our return.*[28] *'They are those upon whom is God's blessing and mercy and they are the ones who are guided."* (2:155-157)

> *"They who are patient, seeking the pleasure of their Lord, who are regular in prescribed prayer, who spend (in charity) secretly and openly out of what God has bestowed on them, and who repel evil with good: for them is the attainment of the final abode."* (13:22)

> *". . . And give good tidings to the humble, whose hearts tremble when God is mentioned and who are patient under that which afflicts them, and who are constant in prescribed*

*prayer and who spend (in charity) out of what We bestow on
them."* (22:34-35)

Indeed, as a rule the sincere believer does not ask God for the
specific outcome of a situation, for he realizes that he cannot
know with certainty what is best for him even in relation to this
life, much less in relation to the hereafter. Rather he asks God to
guide him and make easy for him what is for his good in this
world and in the future life, and to keep him away from whatever is bad or harmful to him in either. For the sincere believer, not
knowing positively himself wherein his good lies, possesses the
assurance that God, Who does know, is able to send good to him
even through the greatest suffering and trial.

Moreover, he has the deep certainty that any trouble, pain or
affliction which he experiences even, as the Prophet (peace be on
him) said, to the pricking of the foot of the believer by a thorn is
an expiation for sins, a source of reward in the hereafter if it is
borne with patience and endurance, and a means of coming nearer to God Most High through that ineffable softening of the heart
which suffering brings through complete trust and reliance upon
Him. In such a situation the sincere believer finds the greatest
solace and comfort of heart in the remembrance of God Most
High, holding fast to Him, depending completely upon Him, and
contemplating His beneficence and exalted glory with words of
praise and adoration in the total surrender of his will and his
being to what He, the Praised and Exalted, sees fit to send. The
Quran speaks of:

*"Those who believe and whose hearts find comfort in the
remembrance of God. Lo! in the remembrance of God do
hearts find comfort."* (13:28)

Thus even trouble and distress constitute great sources of
good to the one whose heart is firmly fixed upon his Lord and
contented with His decree. Such people are often able to remain
uncomplaining, thankful and to experience deep peace of heart
even in the midst of the greatest trials.

Then what does such a person feel about death, either of himself or of a near one? To the sincere believer death is simply the return of the soul to Him Who gave it, the last stage of the journey "from God to God." As such, it holds no terrors for him except the fear that he may not have deserved the pleasure of his Lord, Whose love he desires, Whose anger he dreads, and Whose mercy he hopes for with all his being. The inevitability of death and the hereafter is never far from his consciousness, serving to keep all his life and deeds in perspective as he tries at all times to live in preparedness for what is to come and to send ahead for his soul such deeds as will make heavy his balance of good when he appears before his Lord. And when death claims someone near him, he does not indulge in excesses of grief (for not only does Islam forbid this but its inappropriateness in one who believes is obvious) but prays for God's mercy and peace on the departed, and takes his living and dying as a lesson and example. Islam very strongly emphasizes the distinction between a believer and a nonbeliever, both in terms of their inner state and their true worth. The reason for this may now be apparent. A person devoid of belief and faith and a believer alike are both equally helpless and dependent on the Almighty Power in the universe, of course, but the nonbeliever is either unaware of this or denies, rejects and resents the fact of his servanthood vis-a-vis God. As he does not acknowledge the existence of a Reality other than that which he can perceive or comprehend, insisting on the supremacy of the material world and ascribing to it ultimate value and importance, he does not acknowledge any authority over his life except that of his own desires or the dictates of other human beings or "society."

Such an individual totally lacks accuracy of perspective concerning himself and his life in this world. He is in a state of forgetfulness and heedlessness concerning essential matters, while he preoccupies and busies himself with what is trivial. He is like one rushing blindly, pell-mell, in his intense involvement with the world with material things, activities or pleasures, no matter how shallow and meaningless often in a desperate effort to avoid having to come to grips with the emptiness, restlessness and dissatisfaction inside him which is the natural consequence of his deep alienation from his Creator, himself and the universe he lives in. And yet such individual usually imagines that he is "free" and not the servant of anyone or anything! If we could look into the heart of the sincere believer by way of comparison, we would find an individual at peace and in harmony with his place in the universe, submitting to what God ordains for him and to His guidance willingly, gladly and with awe and fear of his Lord. We would find one who feels at home with all of God's creation because he knows his rightful place in it and hence does not fight with it or try to exploit or harm it.

We would find a person who, in times of trouble, resists disturbing his soul by asking, "Why?" or imagining all he "might have done" to avert it, for he possesses the deep certainty that every circumstance and happening in his life is the result of God's all-wise decree, coming to him as ordained no matter what anyone might or might not do, and that what is required of him in response is patience, steadfastness and complete trust in God. Conversely, if good comes to him, he responds by a profound sense of humility and thankfulness to God from whom it came rather than with pride and preoccupation with his own powers or merits. He maintains a constant perspective within himself: the awareness of the transitory and finite nature of this brief life in comparison with the enduring life of the hereafter, and the desire, which is greater than any other, to attain the good of that life by every means in his power.

Such an individual, by means of this perspective, never loses sight of where he is going or his ultimate goal: to merit God's mercy and pleasure, and thereby to attain the eternal home. As part of the means of attaining it, he is active in the world, taking his responsibilities seriously and trying to fulfill them to the best of his abilities, and being always conscious of his duty to society. But he is not in love with this world and avoids becoming entangled with material preoccupations because there are more important concerns at the center of his life. His constant prayer is, "Our Lord, give us good in this world and good in the hereafter, and save us from the punishment of the fire." To him faith is life itself, without which he could not continue the struggle of existence for one single minute.

> *"...Verily, this world's life is transient, but the hereafter is the permanent abode."* (40:39)

God-consciousness and faith are the two most basic and essential qualities of the one who submits to God's Will and the sincere believer. We will now continue our survey of the qualities and characteristics which Islam enjoins and which it considers essential in an Islamic personality.

SINCERITY

Without this quality the Muslim's relationship with both God and his fellow human being is null and void. Sincerity toward Goal should prompt him to wholeheartedness in worship, to absolute honesty with himself regarding his motives and intentions, and to striving continually to weed out of his character whatever has a trace of hypocrisy, greed, selfishness, envy or the desire for reputation or power, while sincerity toward his fellow human beings should lead him to behave in an open and straightforward manner with them. He should not use or manipulate them for his own purposes, and should genuinely desire their good, liking for them what he likes for himself. He should say what he means, refrain from saying what he does not mean, and should say whatever needs to be said to the other's face rather than behind his back. His relations with others are not to be superficial, casual or careless, and he is expected to interact with everyone responsible sincerely and in a meaningful fashion.

RESPONSIBILITY

This is the keynote of the Muslim's behavior-toward God, toward other human beings, and toward the rest of His creation, both animate and inanimate. His task is first to fulfill his own obligations to God and to other people, regardless of what others may do, and then to try to change, as far as is in his power, whatever he sees that is wrong and evil. His attitude should never be, "Am I my brother's keeper?" but, "I am responsible for doing whatever I can," for he knows that he will be held accountable not only for his own attitudes and actions but for anything else over which he had control or influence in the society and the world around him as well.

INTEGRITY

Because the Muslim has an ever-present consciousness of God and his responsibility to Him, every aspect and act of his life is to be constantly submitted to the standards and criteria of Islam. Nothing is outside the pale of it, from the most private and personal matters to the most public. The standards of Islam are supposed to be so much a part of his very nature that it is difficult for him to knowingly disregard and disobey them in any aspect. And if he does so, his inner attunement to himself and to God's guidance should be so keen that he is at once aware of his mistake and asks for God's forgiveness.

HONESTY, TRUTHFULNESS, KEEPING OF COMMITMENTS, FAIR-DEALING

Since obedience to such principles is basic to mutual trust, responsibility and reliability among human beings as well as to integrity within the personality, these are among the most emphasized qualities in Islam. Such a scrupulous adherence to truth includes absolute honesty and fidelity in all personal relationships and interactions, in business dealings and transactions, and in the administration of justice. The Quran enjoins these qualities over and over again:

> *"O you who believe, be conscious of God and be with the truthful."* (9:119)

> *"(The virtuous are) those Who honor their trusts and promises and those who stand firm in their testimonies . . . ."* (70:32-33)

> *"O you Who believe stand out firmly for justice, bearers*

*of unfitness for God, even though it be against yourselves or
your parents or near relatives. Whether he is rich or poor,
God's claim takes precedence over (the claims of) either of
them. So do not follow your own desires lest you swerve from
justice; and if you lapse or fall away (from truth), then verily,
God is aware of what you do."* (4:135)

*". . . And keep (your) commitments: verily, concerning
commitments (you) will be questioned. Fill the measure when
you measure, and weigh with a right balance: that is good and
right in the end."* (17:34-35)

And among many *hadith* concerning these virtues, the following makes it very clear how essential such qualities are in the
personality of the Muslim.

"There are three characteristics of a hypocrite: when he
speaks he lies, when he makes a promise he acts treacherous-
ly against it, and when he is trusted he betrays."

DISCIPLINE AND SELF-CONTROL

As we have seen, to live the life of a Muslim with its five
daily prayers, month of fasting each year, and obedience to all the
injunctions of Islam, a considerable degree of self-discipline is
needed. This discipline is fostered by the Muslim's continual
awareness that he is not his own master but rather God's slave,
who stands ever ready to hear and to obey his Lord's commands.
Self-control in governing one's temper is very strongly stressed,
and forbearance and making allowances for others' faults are
enjoined. In the case of a personal injury, the Muslim is urged to
forgive and, although retaliation is permitted, to forgo it for the
sake of God out of mercy and compassion to the one who has
wronged him. While Islam discourages asceticism and permits
the enjoyment of God's good gifts, the Muslim is expected to
keep his appetites and desires under control rather than allowing
them to control him. Self-discipline and self-control are reflect-
ed in many aspects of both the private and the public life of

Muslims, from the degree of self-control shown by a Muslim to whom wrong has been done but who keeps his tongue and hand (and with them his heart) from vengefulness, to the orderly and correct manner in which Muslims line themselves up for a congregational prayer.

HUMILITY, PATIENCE, ENDURANCE, COURAGE, THANKFULNESS

The true Muslim is under no illusions about his own greatness or importance; he is humble about his attainments and aware of his own limitations. He does not seek fame or power but rather the pleasure and approval of God, trying to be useful in whatever way he can. As we have seen, he tries to endure unavoidable trouble and suffering patiently and courageously, finding solace and comfort in the remembrance of God, and he is thankful for all good that comes his way. Phrases expressing his dependence on and praise of God form a vital part of his speech patterns.[29] He does not despair in any situation, knowing that everything is possible for God. In any case, the events of this life are not the most important thing to him, but rather to attain God's pleasure and His mercy in the life-to-come.

DIGNITY, HONOR AND SELF-RESPECT

A strong sense of honor and self-respect is an essential quality in the true Muslim. Even the most humble — an illiterate peasant or laborer — often demonstrates a striking degree of uprightness and dignity.

The Muslim's dignity stems from his being the slave of and fearing no one except his Creator; no one can threaten or intimidate him for he knows that what befalls him depends not on other people but on the Lord of the people. Thus he maintains his dignity and serenity even though his life may be full of hardships. His self-respect is the product of the innate straightness of his world-view, concepts and character, and he tries never to do anything which will lower him in his own estimation or that of others — and above all in his Lord's. He realizes that the only real distinction he or any other human being can achieve is due to his degree of God-consciousness, faith and knowledge rather than race, wealth, social status and the like. And as he has his honor, he recognizes and upholds the right of others to theirs, and tries to refrain from behavior which would violate it such as gossiping, prying into people's affairs, being suspicious or interfering with others' privacy.

PURITY, MODESTY AND CHASTITY

To the true Muslim, man and woman alike, anything impure or degrading is abhorrent and to be avoided at all costs. Sexual purity thus begins in the mind of the believer with the fear of God and the desire to maintain that state of inner balance and cleanness which is essential to his or her integrity and well-being. Strict modesty of dress, manner and behavior, and absolute chastity both before and after marriage are required.

KINDNESS, HELPFULNESS, COOPERATION

Islam teaches that human beings are all equally creatures of God, all sharing the same condition. The Muslim's obligation is to live in cooperation, not competition, with his fellow men and to be helpful, kind, just and compassionate toward everyone, regardless of whether they are of the same or a different faith, race, culture or status, etc. Kindness to animals as well as to human beings is required, for abuse or cruelty of any of God's creatures is abhorrent to their Creator. Such virtues are stressed again and again in the Quran and in the Prophet's *hadith*, as for example the following:

> "God still not show mercy to him who does not show mercy to others." (*hadith*)

> The Prophet (peace be on him) said, "I swear by God he does not believe. I swear by God he does not believe. I swear by God he does not believe." He was asked who it was and replied, "The one from whose injurious conduct his neighbor is not safe." (*hadith*)

"The believer is not one who eats his fill when his neighbor beside him is hungry." (*hadith*)

"All creatures are God's children, an those dearest to God are the ones who treat His children kindly." (*hadith*)

CHARITABLENESS, GENEROSITY AND HOSPITALITY

Our brief discussion of *zakah* has already given some idea of how much Islam stresses charitableness and generosity. Indeed, the emphasis is so great that charity is enjoined in verse after verse of the Quran, often together with the obligation of *salah*.

Numerous occasions hare been specified for the giving of charity for example, on the two festivals: as an expiation if one is unable to fast during Ramadan due to pregnancy, suckling an infant, a permanent illness, or old age by feeding one person for each day missed; by remitting a debt to a debtor; or by the ransoming or freeing of captives, etc. This repeated and continuous emphasis on charity in Islam does not allow the Muslim to forget the needs of his brothers and sisters who are less fortunate but to feel them as his own.

But in Islam charity does not consist merely of help to the needy. Rather it includes anything one does which is of good to others. A *hadith* of the Prophet (peace be on him) mentions that charity includes removing thorns from the road and smiling at one's brother. And open-handedness in spending and giving are to be practiced not only towards the poor but also toward one's family, relatives, friends, neighbors, guests, and even strangers. The good things the Muslim has are to be shared, not kept solely for himself. Generosity and hospitality are thus highly-valued qualities among Muslims in every part of the world.

CONSIDERATION AND GOOD MANNERS

Prophet Muhammad (peace be on him) was a living example of the finest and most beautiful manners, and he stressed politeness and consideration as an expression of the Muslim's faith. Basically this means to treat other human beings as they like to be treated and as one likes to be treated oneself, whether they are

Muslims or non-Muslims, relatives, friends, strangers. and even one's enemies.

BROTHERLINESS

In innumerable Quranic verses and *hadith* of the Prophet (peace be on him) we find delineated the nature of the relationship which should exist among Muslims. One's fellow-Muslims are other "selves" for whom the Muslim should desire what he desires for himself and dislike what he dislikes for himself, rejoicing at their good fortune and sharing in their grief. The following are a few well-known *hadith* which convey so expressively the sense of love and brotherliness which Muslims should feel for one another. The Holy Prophet (peace be on him) said:

"I swear by Him in Whose hand is my soul, a person does not believe until he loves for his brother What he loves for himself." (*hadith*)

"You see the believers in their mutual love and affection like one body. When one member has a complaint, the rest of the body is united with it in wakefulness and fever." (*hadith*)

"A Muslim is a Muslim's brother; he does not wrong him or abandon him if anyone cares for his brother's need God will care for his need: if anyone removes one of his brother's anxiety's (hardships), God will remove from him one of the anxieties of the day of resurrection and if anyone conceals a Muslim's secrets (that would disgrace him) God will conceal his secrets on the day of resurrection." (*hadith*)

Observing the interaction among conscientious Muslims, others are often impressed by their warm brotherly or sisterly behavior toward each other, and by the sincerity, openness, kindness and meaningfulness which characterizes their relationships, particularly in contrast to the shallowness and meaninglessness of so much of present day interaction among human beings.

WARMTH AND LOVINGNESS

Although Muslims may be reserved in public, with intimates they are as a rule very warm human beings. This capacity for warmth and affection stems from the love and security which is received in childhood through close relationships with parents and other family members. This is expressed in cheerfulness, good-temper, a sense of humor, loyalty in relationships, very warm ties with family and friends, love for children, and consideration for other people and their feelings.

STRIVING AND HARD WORK

The Quran states that "*The human being shall have nothing but what he strives for*" (53:39), and there are numerous hadith enjoining and encouraging working and striving in the worldly realm. Muslims are expected to develop their skills and talents, and to utilize and manage the earth's resources: however, this is to be done in a manner which is for the benefit of society and in keeping with the Islamic goals and values. It is also a fundamental responsibility of Muslims to try to shape the conditions of society and the world for good, and to contribute their utmost to the welfare of their communities.

LOVE OF KNOWLEDGE

The Prophet (peace be on him) proclaimed that seeking knowledge is a duty on every Muslim man and woman, and indeed the love of knowledge has been a characteristic of Muslims from the earliest times. As a result, as history attests, at a time when Europe was still extremely primitive and undeveloped, Muslims possessed highly-developed science, mathematics, medicine and literature. Knowledge and understanding are among the most important characteristics of a true Muslim, for without them his Islam is likely to be mere imitation and he will lack the ability to manage the affairs of his society and the world, or even of his own family, in a correct and appropriate manner.

IV.
ISLAMIC MORALS AND BEHAVIOR

" *The (true) servants of the Merciful are those who walk on the earth in humility, and when the ignorant address them, they say, 'Peace'; those who pass the night prostrating themselves and standing before their Lord, and those who say: 'Our Lord, avert from us the torment of hell; indeed, the torment of it is anguish and indeed, it is evil as an abode and station.' And those who, when they spend, are neither extravagant nor miserly; for between them (these extremes) is a just course. And those who do not call upon any other deity with God, and do not take a life which God has made sacred except in the way of justice, nor commit adultery and whoever does this will pay the penalty. . . . And those who do not witness falsehood, and when they pass by what is rain pass by with honor; and those who, when they are reminded of the revelations of their Lord, do not fall down deaf and blind thereat; and who say, 'Our Lord, grant us comfort in our spouses and our offspring, and make us examples for those who are God-conscious.' They will be awarded a place in heaven because they were patient, and they will meet therein with welcome and peace, abiding there (forever). Beautiful is it as an abode and station!*" (25:63-68, 72-76)

It cannot be stressed strongly enough that Islam is not a mere

99

belief system nor a "religion" in the commonly understood sense of the word. Rather it is what in Arabic is called a *deen*: a total frame of reference, a complete system and way of life which embraces the entirety of the human being's existence. It does not separate what pertains to "religion," such as acts of worship, from what pertains to human interaction and mundane or "secular" life. Consequently there is no fragmentation or division within the personality of the Muslim due to the splitting of life into compartments or applying different rules or criteria to different parts of life. The same divine system, the same God-given laws and standards govern all aspects of life, and all of an individual's actions are considered by Islam as worship in the broad sense of the term if they are done with the sincere intention of pleasing God in keeping with His injunctions.

Neither is Islam a vague, amorphous religion which is satisfied with merely asking people to be kind, good and morally upright. It is clear and specific about matters which are prohibited (*haram*), as well as about those which are obligatory (*fard*), and about these there is no question. Among permissible (*halal*) things there are degrees, with classifications such as "meritorious," "detestable" or "neutral." The guide for the Muslim's conduct in all spheres of his life is, first, the Holy Quran and, second, the Prophet's example or practice (the *sunnah*, which relates to what he himself did, recommended or approved of in others, and the *Hadith*, which records the *sunnah*). Hence the Muslim does not have to grope about or to wonder if a given behavior is good or bad. If it is bad it will be prohibited by a clear text either in the Quran or the *Hadith*; otherwise, in general, if no text exists in either of these prohibiting it, it is not because God forgot but because He did not intend to prohibit it because in His knowledge it is not harmful.

Although this is a very complex subject which is beyond the scope of this book, it is important to mention that besides being the guide for the individual Muslim's conduct, the Quran and the *sunnah* also constitute the sources of Islamic legislation known as the *shariah*. From this vast body of principles has been derived the system of Islamic jurisprudence (*fiqh*) which deals with all aspects of life, both individual and collective. The Hanafi, Hanbali, Maliki, Shafii and Jafari *madhab*s are actually various schools of Islamic jurisprudence, not separate sects within Islam, as many people erroneously believe.[30]

The principles governing morals and behavior in Islam can be stated as follows. First, everything is permissible except what the Law Giver, God Himself, has clearly prohibited either in the Quran or the Prophet's *sunnah*, which is a practical interpretation of the Quran. No human being can claim or is entitled to the authority to make something permissible or prohibited, for this authority belongs to God alone. Accordingly, attempting to make something prohibited which is permissible, and vice-versa, is tantamount to *shirk*, that is, ascribing divinity to something other than God because the authority and the right to legislate morals and behavior belongs to God alone.

Another principle of Islamic law is that whatever leads to prohibited things is itself prohibited. Moreover, what is doubtful or equivocal should be avoided lest it eventually involve one in what is unlawful, and one should not place himself in situations of temptation or approach near to what is prohibited. Playing with God's injunctions and resorting to trickery or deceit to make the unlawful seem permissible is also obviously prohibited. Good intentions are not an excuse for doing what is unlawful; a good end does not justify a wrong means in Islam. And what is unlawful is unlawful for everyone without regard to sex, status, wealth or any other criterion whatsoever, for in Islam things are not forbidden to the ordinary citizen but allowed to "special" people, or permitted to men but forbidden to women; the head of state, the most eminent religious scholar and the lowliest beggar, and every man as well as every woman, alike are subject to the same laws. Finally, unlawful things may be treated as lawful for a very temporary period and subject to extremely strict rules in the case of very urgent, compelling necessity. For example, although the eating of pork is strictly prohibited, if one is without food of any kind to the point of starvation, he may resort to the consumption of pork, but only in that minimal amount which

meets his bare needs and without any greed or desire for the prohibited thing.

The laws given by God for guidance of human beings are
moral and spiritual principles just as vital and binding as the natural laws which He has ordained for the physical universe, and
just as certain in their operation. And God's laws, whether for the
human being or for the rest of the natural world, are never whim-
sical or arbitrary but rather the result of His infinite knowledge of
what is for the good of His creatures. Indeed, He has prohibited
only those things which are injurious or undesirable for human
beings. Thus the fundamental principle governing Islamic morals
and behavior is that whatever is beneficial is permitted and whatever is harmful to the human being that is, whatever degrades
him, lowers his dignity as a human being, hurts his body, mind or
soul, or is injurious to his society is prohibited.

Only Almighty God can possess the omniscient wisdom to
know in absolute terms what is beneficial and what is harmful for
the life of human individuals and their society, since people, even
the wisest or best of them, are bound by a limited human understanding and perspective. In any case, if something is prohibited,
many harmless and beneficial alternatives have been provided
among permissible things in its place, thus enabling human
beings to satisfy their needs and desires without resorting to
impure, harmful or injurious things or behaviors.

Now what precisely are the Islamic teachings relating to
morals and behavior? In many respects they resemble the teachings of Judaism and Christianity, a fact which one would naturally expect since the messages brought by Moses, Jesus,
Muhammad and all the other prophets (peace be on them all),
who are referred to in the Quran as "*muslims*," that is, those who
submit to God, was one and the same: the message of surrender
to God's will and guidance. But the Islamic teachings, as we shall
see, go many steps further, embracing the whole of individual and
collective life in all its aspects personal, social, political and economic, as well as what pertains to the spiritual life thus providing
alike for the needs of his body, mind and soul. They include the
rights which an individual owes to himself, the rights which he
owes to God, and the rights which he owes to others. In many

ways the Islamic teachings are also far more clear and specific. Rather than merely laying down broad general principles such as, "Be kind" or "Be honest," clear illustrations provided in the Quran and in the Prophet's *sunnah* demonstrate what being kind and honest mean in practical terms; that is, the concrete behaviors appropriate to various situations which embody the virtues which Islam inculcates in the Muslim's personality are clearly defined and delineated.

Islam proclaims that the guidance contained in the Quran is final, permanent and binding on all people of all times and places. Consequently, regardless of how much time may pass and to what extent the habits and living patterns of people may change, the principles of Islam, its standards, values and injunctions are not subject to change no matter what the prevalent values of the society or the opinion of the majority may happen to be. In Islam the consensus of the majority or the desires of people can never alter a divine principle or law, or make right wrong or wrong right, for this is the prerogative of God alone. This does not, of course, in any sense imply that Islam is against change or that it wants a static society, but it does mean that its laws for governing human behavior constitute permanent and unalterable spiritual principles within the framework of which the human being is to order his life; as such, they are not time-bound nor subject to alteration. Thus, while there may naturally be vast changes in people's life-styles and ways of doing things with the passing of time, the principles and laws of Islam may not be altered, "modernized," "reformed" or in any way made conformable to the desires of the people since they come from the Lord of the people, not for their pleasure or convenience but for their permanent well-being and utmost good.

In order to put the Islamic teachings relating to morals and behavior into a clearer perspective, we have listed below a number of Islamic injunctions and prohibitions. Obeying the injunctions is considered a virtue, while doing what is prohibited constitutes disobedience to God and a sin. As will be seen, there is considerable overlapping between the values/attitudes we discussed in the preceding section, and morals and their actualization in behavior. Taken all together, this should enable us to build a clear understanding of the kind of person Islam wants the Muslim to be, what moral principles it wants him to live by, and how it wants him to behave.

It will be clear from the following how far-reaching and comprehensive the Islamic moral injunctions are, applying just as much to the social, political, legal, administrative and economic affairs of the Muslim society as they do to the individual Muslim's relationship with God or with his family and friends. This is because Islam views human life as an indivisible, unified whole which cannot be broken up into unrelated parts. Consequently, notions such as "the separation of church and state" or "rendering unto God what is God's and unto Caesar what is Caesar's" do not fit and have no relevance when applied to Islam, for they pertain to a religion or ideology in which the various elements of life are considered to be separate from each other, with different criteria applied to each. In Islam there is no church establishment, no priesthood (for the Islamic scholars, religion teachers, *imams* and other religious functionaries are simply persons who are well-versed in Islamic knowledge, not priests; they are not ordained or regarded as divinely-appointed, or as having any special or intermediary status with God), and no notion of one part of life being for God and the hereafter and another part being for the world, since all of the human being's life is for God and for Him alone.

What the Islamic teachings actually accomplish is to make the human being into an integrated, unified being, giving his life the form and direction which its Creator wants it to have. The Quran tells us that although the human being has been created in the best of molds and his nature is higher than even that of the angels, in order to reach this potential he must submit to God's guidance and strive to his utmost. The function of the Islamic teachings, therefore, is to work with the human being's extremely complex, multi-faceted nature, with its components of body, mind and soul, and bring it under one jurisdiction, so to speak. Instead of either denying the animal part of the human being or suppressing it altogether, or alternatively allowing it unlimited freedom, Islam directs and channelizes such needs and desires so that they can be expressed in a manner which is constructive and beneficial rather than in a random, uncontrolled manner which can destroy the human being and his society. For example, Islam does not condemn or deny the human being's sexual needs but insists that expressions of human sexuality be limited to a particular use under specified conditions: that is, only in the married state as part of a total relationship of mutual commitment and responsibility. Again, it takes another basic element of human nature, the desire for gain and material possessions, establishing such limits and direction for it as will keep the Muslim from losing his perspective and becoming greedy, miserly, self-indulgent or preoccupied with material things. Islam insists, in short, that the human being be truly human, not an animal or a devil who has lost all sense of perspective in the pursuit of his uncontrolled, undirected aims and desires.

Commands and Injunctions	**Prohibitions**
Consciousness and fear of God (*taqwa*) are to govern all a Muslim's behavior; the acts of worship are a means to this end.	A Muslim is never supposed to lose sight of his relationship and responsibility to God nor to act in violation of it.
Self-discipline and self-control are essential to a Muslim's character and behavior.	Undisciplined desires, over-indulgence in physical appetites and luxuries, uncontrolled passions, harshness and a bad temper are considered detestable.
Truthfulness, reliability and honesty, both in character and in behavior, and the keeping of promises, commitments and trusts are required.	Lying, cheating, failing to keep promises and trusts, and any type of dishonest dealing are strictly prohibited.
To be just and fair, even at the expense of one's own self or one's family is required on an individual level. Islamic society is also required to adhere very strictly to justice in all affairs.	Injustice and unfairness in any form are very strongly condemned. Islamic society is not permitted to perpetrate injustice upon human beings in any form.

Commands and Injunctions

All human life is sacred to Muslims and upholding its sanctity is an Islamic obligation, however Muslims have the right to equal retaliation (to be applied by the state).

Forgiveness for personal injuries inflicted by others is enjoined. If the injured person or his immediate relatives choose not to forgive, however, they have the right to retaliation. This is not to exceed the injury done and is not to be inflicted upon anyone except the guilty person himself. A monetary settlement is also acceptable in place of physical retaliation.

A Muslim is supposed to resist injustice, tyranny and oppression, both of himself and others, by every means in his power: with his hand, with his tongue, and within his heart.

Respect for the property and possessions of others, as for one's own, is required. In a society in which *zakah* is in effect, and where widespread voluntary charity is practiced, stealing due to poverty becomes unnecessary and criminal.

Purity, modesty and decency in behavior, appearance, dress and speech are required. The dignity and honor of women is very strongly stressed. Marriage is very much encouraged, providing a permissible and sanctioned outlet for sexual needs.

Prohibitions

Killing except in self-defense or in a righteous war is one of the greatest sins. Life may be taken by the state only after due process of law for capital crimes.

Revenge and blood-feuding are prohibited and are considered serious sins. Equal retaliation constitutes justice while revenge is a willful transgression of justice and defiance of the authority of the law.

Tyranny and oppression of any of God's creatures, including by a ruler or government, are very strictly prohibited and constitute very grave sins.

Stealing is prohibited and is severely punished. However, the punishment is to be applied only in cases of deliberate theft, not theft due to hunger or want.

Free mixing between men and women and any form of physical contact outside marriage are prohibited. A woman's beauty and sexual attributes are not for public display. Fornication, adultery, prostitution and homosexuality are not merely personal sins but also very serious crimes which attack the foundations of a wholesome society.

Commands and Injunctions

Prohibitions

Responsible and harmonious relations between husband and wife, proper care, maintenance and training of children are stressed.

Lack of responsibility, cruelty or harshness toward one's spouse or children are condemned.

Obedience, respect and kind treatment of parents, and kindly, responsible relations with relatives are of the greatest importance.

Disobedience, dishonor or harshness toward parents are among the worst of sins. Breaking ties of relationship with kin is prohibited.

Neighborliness, helpfulness and kindliness in all spheres of life and to all people are enjoined.

Hard-heartedness, unkindness and bad behavior to others are detested.

Respect for the honor, reputation and privacy of others is required.

Gossiping, back-biting, prying into others' affairs, suspicion, violating others' privacy are prohibited.

Kindness to animals, respect for all of God's creation are enjoined. If an animal is to be killed, it must be done swiftly and in a merciful manner.

Torture or cruelty to animals of any kind, killing animals for sport and wanton destruction of nature are prohibited.

Ownership of property, trade and business are permissible and encouraged. Money is to remain in circulation through useful investment or spending. Work and constructive effort of all kinds are encouraged.

Gaining wealth by interest, bribery or gambling is prohibited. Society is to flourish through cooperation and mutual help, not by the exploitation of some people by others. Any economic practice which harms people or society, including working in prohibited trades is forbidden.

Spending in a reasonable manner on oneself or one's family is permissible. Generosity and hospitality are strongly enjoined. The right of the poor and distressed on one's wealth is to be remembered.

Excessive love of wealth or possessions, miserliness, hoarding, spending for unreasonable luxuries and wastefulness are all prohibited. Material things are not to become a preoccupation or one's goal in life.

Commands and Injunctions

Enjoyment, in moderation, of God's wholesome gifts of food and drink is permissible.

Prohibitions

Gluttony and over-indulgence in food or drink are disliked. The use of alcohol, intoxicating drugs and pork is prohibited.

Cooperation for good, enjoining what is right and forbidding what is wrong, are obligations. The Muslim of any walk of life or calling is to feel a sense of responsibility for the state of his society and its affairs.

Cooperating for evil purposes is prohibited and lack of concern or failure to try to change what is wrong are breaches of responsibility.

An aerial view of the Sacred Mosque in Mecca. The black-draped Ka'aba stands in its center.

The Holy Ka'aba, surrounded by pilgrims performing tawaf *(near center) and* salat.

A group of pilgrims makes its supplications to God upon entering the Sacred Mosque.

A view of the vast tent city at Mina during hajj.

The castle and mosque of Muhammad 'Ali Bey in Cairo.

A group of Muslims in America performing congregational salat.

A section of Istanbul.

Bright-eyed Arab kindergarten pupils stand up to greet a visitor.

Mosaic ornamentation in the Jum'a Mosque, Isfahan, Iran.

Interior of the Prophet's Mosque, Medina.

Selimiye Mosque, Edirne, Turkey, a masterpiece of Islamic architecture built during the sixteenth century.

The interior of Selimiye Mosque, Edirne.

A village in Jordan.

Muhabat Khan's Mosque, Peshawar, Pakistan.

An American Muslim family.

A section of the Omayyad Mosque, Damascus.

PART THREE:
THE COLLECTIVE ASPECT

V.
ISLAM IN SOCIETY

Our next step will be to take a look at how the Islamic teachings are applied to the collective aspects of human life. It is not our intention here to either discuss any existing societies or to set up a model for an Islamic society, but simply to convey some idea of how Islam regulates various aspects of human interaction and to make some observations as to how this may be implemented in practice.

As we have already seen, Islam possesses its own social, political, legal and economic concepts and systems, all of which have their base in the Quran and the Prophet's *sunnah*. While these may have some points of similarity to the concepts and systems of other societies or ideologies, they are in fact unique and distinctive to Islam and cannot be forced into the mold of this or that man-made system or philosophy.

It is important to bear in mind that by the time the revelation of the Quran had been completed in the year 632 AD, the principles governing these concepts and systems had been laid down in complete form. Hence the Islamic concepts and systems — whether they relate to political, economic, legal or social aspects — pre-date the development of modern systems in any part of the world by several hundred years. Any apparent similarities between Islam and other systems cannot, therefore, possibly be due to Islam's "borrowing" from them but rather to the "borrowing" of other systems from Islam, or, more logically, to the fact that Islam's principles and laws are so obviously correct and workable that they would ultimately have been discovered by thinkers in other systems with or without any borrowing having taken place. In actual fact, the similarities between the Islamic principles and other systems are more apparent than real, for unless a system is firmly rooted in acknowledgment of the Creator, acceptance of the human being's accountability to Him, and simultaneous recognition of His sole right to legislate for His creatures and their obligation to obey Him, the resemblance of any concept or system to Islam is obviously a superficial one.

The point to be borne in mind is that the principles on which the Islamic systems are based are constant, unalterable and universal ones originating in divine revelation. However, the details of their application may certainly be adjusted as necessary within the Islamic framework to fit existing needs and circumstances. Hence, while Muslims are unquestionably permitted to adopt useful and beneficial knowledge and technology from any source, they are not to do this blindly. In concrete terms, if they make use of a technology from a non-Islamic source, they are permitted to accept only the technology itself, not the concepts, values or behavior of the society from which it originates, nor anything related to its application which is contrary to Islamic values and laws. The technology, which is a practical, concrete thing, is then assimilated into the total Islamic framework of the society, acquiring its own Islamic emphasis and perspective so that it can be a source of benefit, not of harm or disruption of values and societal patterns. For the mission of the Islamic society is not to imitate others' concepts, life-styles or habits but rather to be the leader and example to other societies, particularly in the area of spiritual and moral values.

*****

In discussing the collective aspects of human interaction in any society, it is only logical to start at the beginning—that is, with the family. The Islamic teachings are designed to strengthen and protect this precious nurturing ground of future generations with the utmost care and concern. However, in Islam "family" does not denote merely the nuclear family of Western society but includes, in addition to husband, wife and children, other close relatives as well. This of course does not mean that all the relatives must live together under one roof or even near each other but that, even if they are scattered and geographically distant, they recognize their membership in a unit whose numbers are bound together by ties of blood and mutual responsibility.

In Islam marriage, which is the cornerstone of the family, is very strongly encouraged; in fact, it is mentioned in a *hadith* of the Prophet (peace be on him) as being the second half or completion of one's faith. The purpose of marriage in Islam is that a man and woman build a home, live together in love, kindness, mutual sympathy, support and companionship, meet one another's sexual needs, and rear children together. By their marriage they form a new family unit which also supports and strengthens the existing families of the pair. Marriage is seen as a working partnership, with each partner assuming responsibility for their common life together.

Islam recognizes that men and women have different natures, strengths and weaknesses, and hence it assigns different but complementary roles within the society to each, dividing the total work which must be done for the process of living between them in a way which best suits their innate capacities and natures. Within the family group, Islam assigns the leadership role to men, together with financial responsibility for its members; the support and maintenance of the women and children are their concern. Women in turn are responsible for looking after their husbands' comfort and well-being, guarding their honor and administering their properties, providing for the physical and emotional well-being of their children, and, with their husbands' help rearing them in the best possible way as sound Muslims. Although as a matter of convenience most women do the work of their households, this is not required by Islam, and a woman is perfectly free to turn over all or part of the domestic work to others, as circumstances permit, and to pursue her own work or interests, provided the family—particularly in the area of the training of children—is not neglected.

Islam lays great stress on the importance and desirability of having children and makes raising them properly a matter of vital concern. At the same time, young people are required to develop a sense of responsibility for their own conduct quite early in life. A young Muslim is considered by Islam as accountable for his or her own actions by the age of puberty (that is, by the age of eleven to sixteen years), by which time an individual is considered to be capable of possessing an adequate understanding of the Islamic teachings and of what is permissible and prohibited, as well as a sound practice of its various aspects. Children are reared with the understanding that the values and behaviors they are taught are not simply their parents' but God's, and that they apply as much to their parents and all other members of society as to themselves, while the parents for their part are expected to provide a sound example for them to follow. Consequently there is a continuity of values from generation to generation, and rebellion against them is not merely a rebellion against parental standards but against God. As a result, while the drive for independence naturally exists among maturing Muslim youth, rather than being a time of crisis, rebellion or deviation from accepted norms, adolescence is rather a time for serious preparation and adjustment to the assumption of adult responsibility.

Islam also requires that Muslims take responsibility for their parents when they become elderly or for other aged relatives who may need their care or support. In an Islamic society, the phenomenon of a single woman or old person living alone is virtually unknown; such people are to be part of someone's household where their material wants and need for love, care and companionship can be met in a humane manner. Women's right to maintenance by the men of their families (their husbands, or if they are single, widowed or divorced, their fathers, brothers, adult sons or some other male relative) protects them from having to go out and struggle to earn a living the best they can, although they may lack marketable skills and work opportunities compatible with the dignity of women, in addition to the problem of the care and rearing of their children. Muslim women may own property, engage in business or work, but even in this case they are not required to provide for the family's maintenance because Islam has made this the responsibility of men.

Partly in order to provide a home and maintenance for every woman in the society and partly in order to make provision for other special situations, Islam permits Muslim men to marry more than one wife. This provision for limited polygamy is not, as some imagine, a recommendation or encouragement to plural marriage, or a blanket permission to marry more than one woman and then treat the wives any way one likes. Rather the permission to contract marriage with more than one woman is contingent upon the observance of scrupulous fairness among the wives. In the words of the Quran:

> '"And if you fear that you will not deal justly by orphans, marry of the women who seem good to you two or three or four. And if you fear that you cannot do justice, then another. . . . " (4 :3)

> "You will not be able to deal equally between wives how- ever much you desire (to do so). But (if you have more than one wife) do not turn altogether away (from one), leaving her as in suspense . . . .'" (4:129)

This does not of course mean that a man must love his wives equally—an obvious impossibility since no one can order his emotions—but that he should provide them with equal facilities and maintenance, spend an equal amount of time with each, and not give them the feeling that he prefers one over the other. This is clearly no easy task for the average man. Yet because Islam recognizes the nature and needs of women, and does not want them to live alone to bear all the economic and other burdens of life on their shoulders, or to spend their lives without the love and care of a husband or the blessing of children; because it takes into cognizance that there are unusual situations such as barrenness or chronic illness in women which might make marrying more than one wife desirable, the permission for plural marriages has been given.

For example, after a war the number of women is often much

greater than that of men and many women are helpless and destitute. The Islamic solution—the humane, dignified and natural
solution is that a man should, under such conditions, shoulder the
responsibility for more than one wife and provide for these
homeless ones rather than their being forced to struggle alone in
order to survive, often being reduced to prostitution because they
can find no other means of livelihood. While it is unfortunately
true that in practice the Islamic provision for polygamy has
sometimes been misused, this does not change the wisdom of this
provision, the result of which in past times was to stabilize
Muslim societies by making it possible for every single individual to marry and have a home in one way or another. Moreover,
with such a provision there is no excuse for anyone—man or
women—to resort to illicit relationships to satisfy his/her sexual
needs. However, no matter how fair a husband may try to be with
his wives, there are obvious problems of rivalry and jealousy in
plural marriages, and thus, while the provision for polygamy
makes the social system flexible enough to deal with all kinds of
conditions, it is not necessarily recommended or preferred by
Islam.[31]

While divorce is allowed, the Prophet (peace be on him) said
that of all the things which God has permitted, divorce is the
most hated by Him. This in itself points to the grave undesirability of divorce except as a last resort when all means of reconciliation between husband and wife fail. Such means include the
attempts of relatives and friends to mediate between the two to
help them resolve their differences. Effective safeguards are also
built into the divorce procedure so that at any stage short of the
final pronouncement reconciliation between the two parties can
take place. When divorce does occur, however, it is not hedged
about by difficulties or by long-drawn-out court procedures with
mutual recriminations or fights over the custody of children, nor
is a human being penalized by having to support his former wife
for the remainder of his life even though he may not have been
at fault in any way. In any case, divorce is in fact an infrequent
occurrence among Muslims. Although the two partners as a rule
do not know each other before marriage since Islam totally pro-

hibits such things as dating or pre-marital intimacy, the fact that Muslim marriages are based on common beliefs, values, ways of life and submission to God's commands rather than on romantic attachment before marriage provides them with a strong and sound foundation for building a life together.

As we have seen, absolute chastity before marriage and absolute fidelity to one's mate is required of both men and women. Islam considers the honor of women sacred and insists that they be treated with appropriate dignity and respect, and for their part they are required to guard their modesty and purity with utmost care. An Islamic society is to be free of the degradation of women and the exploitation of their sexuality, whether by men or by commercial interests, and of any influences which weaken marriage, the family or peoples' morals. Thus Islam establishes certain limits to govern the relations between men and women so that the interaction of Muslims may be characterized by absolute integrity, openness, purity and honesty.

Muslims traditionally address one another as "brother" and "sister" and attempt to behave as befits such a relationship. Responsibility may be said to be the keynote of all relationships and interaction among them, and the rights of others and one's obligations toward them are universally acknowledged. Cooperation is the rule rather than competition; in fact, competition should consist of trying to excel in being and doing good rather than in outdoing others in acquiring possessions, status or other such aspects of life. Unity of purpose and action, mutual helpfulness and working together are very strongly stressed.

In Islam helpfulness and concern for others preclude such practices as dealing in interest which takes advantage of others' needs and permits an increase in the wealth of the lender of money without his working for it, whether it is done by an individual or a financial institution such as a bank, and Muslims are expected to develop and implement a sound, workable alternative interest-free economic system. Neither are any sorts of commercial interests permitted to exploit the people, whether it be by exciting greed and materialism through advertising, by the manufacture of goods which are harmful or undesirable, or by ecologically unsound practices which wantonly destroy irreplaceable natural resources for easily dispensed with consumer goods. Wastage, whether of wealth or of natural resources, is prohibited; instead, the resources given by God are to be treated with respect and utilized in the best way possible for the welfare of all, with an eye to the future as well as the present.

The material development of the society, whether by industrialization, utilization of resources, the application of science and technology, or other means is considered a religious obligation in Islam. However, the aim of all such efforts must be the welfare of the people and the society, keeping in mind the needs of future generations as well, never the enrichment of individuals or interest groups. Hence new developments under consideration in an Islamic society might be studied by panels of experts in various fields, including Islamic sociologists and psychologists, to determine their probable long-range effects on the society, and they would be undertaken or dropped on the basis of their recommendations. Random and too rapid development, which destroys religious and societal values and stable living patterns, would not be permitted, and moderation in production and consumption patterns would be stressed.

The charitableness which is so central to the feeling of love and brotherhood among Muslims is intended to equalize the wealth in the society so that some people are not excessively rich while others are destitute. Every Muslim is expected to feel and to accept responsibility for those who are near to him, and even for others who are outside his immediate circle. Thus orphans are as a rule brought up by relatives, not adopted by strangers or put into institutions, and as we have mentioned, a similar responsibility is assumed for the aged and for single, widowed or divorced women, either by their relatives or through plural marriages.

To put it another way, in the Islamic society, kindness, charitableness and help to the needy and unfortunate are personalized rather than institutionalized; that is, such help is not merely the duty of the government but is the responsibility of every Muslim toward whomever is within his reach as far as his means allows

although the government is required to do its part by collecting
and distributing *zakah* and by any additional means, such as the
levying of taxes and duties, it may consider necessary.

In any group of two or more Muslims, one is selected by
them as the leader; this applies not only to a group which has
gathered for *salah* and to the family but to any collection of individuals, including the Islamic society and state. Since the people
have deputed authority to the leader, they have the obligation to
follow his leadership and instructions even if they disagree with
him,[32] provided he does not ask them to do anything which
involves disobedience to God. However, if he does not fulfill his
responsibilities, does not follow the teachings of Islam either in
his personal life or in the conduct of the affairs of state, or asks
the people to disobey God's laws, he must be replaced by a more
responsible person. In Islam the leader or head of state has no
special prerogatives or privileges but rather only graver responsibilities for which he will be held accountable to God; he is in
office not for his own aggrandizement but to serve the people. He
is therefore required to consult with the people and to consider
their needs and well-being in all matters.[33] An Islamic government therefore embodies the dual principles of obedience to the
leader and the leader's obligation to consult with the people concerning the conduct of affairs.[34] Moreover, no legislation is to be
enacted which is contrary to the Quran or the Prophet's *sunnah*,
and all legislation which is enacted is to be in conformity with
these two sources of Islamic legislation. In matters concerning
which Islam is silent, the government is of course free to enact
whatever legislation it deems necessary within the general framework of the laws and values of Islam.

An Islamic government is responsible for providing an environment which will make it easy for Muslims to practice Islam
and difficult for them to deviate from it. Any establishments
which thrive on immoral or prohibited activities such as those
related to prostitution and other forms of sexual license. gambling, drinking, etc., would not be permitted; manufacture and
sale of alcoholic beverages, drug traffic and pornographic literature would be illegal; and the public media would not be allowed

to portray or describe anything leading toward sexual immorality, vice and crime. In principle, an wholesome and permissible outlets and recreations which do not conflict with Islamic goals and values would be encouraged and proper facilities for them provided. The modesty and dignity of women would be safeguarded by encouraging modest dress, providing separate facilities wherever necessary (secondary schools and colleges, medical and recreational facilities, etc.), and taking stern measures against those who in any way annoy or molest women.

Seeking knowledge is considered a religious obligation in Islam, and education for both children and adults would be strongly stressed. Schools would combine secular and Islamic studies into one curriculum through secondary level in order to provide a comprehensive and integrated approach. A very broad-based religious education would be included which would not only offer Islamic studies but the study of other religions, systems, ideologies and cultures. A sense of pride in one's Islamic identity and heritage would be stressed. Young people would be given assistance in marrying early if they desired so that their sexual needs could be met without resort to illicit relations. Preparation and training for parenthood would be made available to them, and parents would be given every support and assistance in rearing their children properly. Women would be encouraged to obtain higher education to prepare them both to be effective homemakers and mothers and for other essential work, particularly in the educational, medical, nursing and social work fields, and accommodations in schedule and leave would be made for working women to enable them to take care of the needs of their families and for such situations as pregnancy, childbirth, illness in the family, etc.

Justice before the law would be strictly impartial without regard to religion, race, position, wealth or any other criteria; the head of state, officials and members of the most influential families would be just as subject to its provisions as the most humble members of society. In this context it may be remarked that every individual in a society has a certain basic responsibility to that society not to transgress against its established limits, which relate to the sanctity of life, person, property and sexual inviolability. In turn each society has its own system of penalties for violating such limits which stem from its basic understanding of human responsibility and interaction. In a society in which the majority of people are Muslims, that is, accepting the limits laid down by Almighty God, crimes would be dealt with by the punishments prescribed by Islam.[35] Islam maintains that the violation of these limits, which are known to all, calls for such exemplary punishment that others will be effectively deterred from committing similar acts.

Freedom of religion and conscience for non-Muslims living in the Islamic state is a fundamental principle of Islam, including the freedom to practice the rites of their respective faiths. The Quran commands explicitly, "*Let there be no compulsion in religion*" (2:256), for one's religious beliefs are obviously a matter of inner conviction and cannot be imposed from outside, nor does anyone have the right to impose them since God gives each human individual freedom to choose them for himself.[36] Islam also guarantees all other basic freedoms to all persons in an Islamic state without any distinction or discrimination on the basis of religion, race, national origin, etc. In such a state every citizen would be guaranteed such rights as protection of person, property and honor, justice before the law on an equal basis with all other citizens, ownership of private property, the right to engage in business or investment beneficial to society, to select his/her own marriage partner, to acquire an education, to travel, and to do any lawful work of his own choice.

Although the head of the Islamic state would by definition be a Muslim, non-Muslims would be guaranteed adequate representation and would be able to hold positions of importance in the society. Non-Muslims, like Muslims themselves, would obviously not be permitted to carry on activities which are prohibited or undermining to morals and social stability, and no one would be permitted to propagate atheism or godless, violent ideologies such as communism or to engage in political activities related to them.

As has already been mentioned, *jihad* is an obligation on the individual Muslim, and it is an obligation on the Islamic society as well. Unfortunately the word *jihad* has been represented so often in the Western media (and by some well-meaning but ignorant Muslims as well) as meaning "holy war" that this is now accepted as its real meaning. This is totally incorrect, for *jihad* simply means "striving," as any native speaker of Arabic can verify. The first and most essential *jihad* which the Muslim must carry on is within himself in a never ceasing effort at self-improvement and self-purification. This is known as *jihad bil nafs* (striving within the self), which the Prophet, peace be on him, called "the greater *jihad*." This unremitting struggle is to begin within the Muslim's soul from the time he or she attains a consciousness of right and wrong, and it does not end until the end of life itself.

In addition to this, Islam makes it a duty on Muslims to reach out into society and carry on the struggle, by any means in their power both on an individual and collective level, against all forms of evil and corruption; they are also required to wage an unremitting war on injustice, tyranny and oppression. Such *jihad fi sabeel* Allah (striving in the path of God) is to be carried on by the tongue, by the pen, and, if these fail, by the hand as a last resort. Islam absolutely prohibits Muslims to perpetrate injustice, aggression or harm on others: it also enjoins forgiveness and forbearance in the case of personal wrongs done to themselves. At the same time, they are not permitted to allow themselves or others to become the passive victims of others' injustice or aggression which, if they are not checked, will become more and more menacing to human dignity and freedom. The Quran says:

> *"Permission is given to those who fight because they have been wronged, and indeed God is able to give them victory: those who have been driven from their homes unjustly only because they said, 'Our Lord is God.' For had it not been for God's repelling some people by means of others, cloisters and churches and oratories and mosques, in which the name of God is often mentioned, would assuredly have been pulled*

*down. And lo! God helps one who helps Him. For verily, God
is Strong, Powerful."* (22:39-40),

A *hadith* of the Prophet (peace be on him) further clarifies
this point. He instructed some of his companions, "Help your
brother, whether he is the oppressor or the oppressed." When
they asked him how they could help one who was an oppressor,
he said, "Restrain him from it." Thus the Muslim is not only
required to give assistance to one who is the victim of tyranny,
injustice and wrong-doing, whether is a Muslim or a non-
Muslim, a single individual or a whole people, but also to try to
stop the one who is committing it and to strive with all his energies to bring about the rule of righteousness, freedom and justice
for all people.

*****

A society such as the one we have just finished describing
would be one which, if it existed, would be as nearly ideal in
moral and human terms as it is possible for a society to be. It
would long ago have won the admiration of all sincere and concerned people and would have attained the moral leadership of
the world. The question may now rightly be asked, "Where is
such a society? If Islam is all you say it is, why don't we see societies like this throughout the Muslim world? Doesn't this prove
that Islam cannot be all you say? Besides this, we know some
Muslims. Perhaps a very few of them may be something like
what you have described but the rest are just regular people not
especially good in any way or even really different from other
people, and some of them are even worse. In the face of all the
claims and counter-claims we are hearing today about Islam, how
can we know whether what you are saying is correct or what the
critics and opponents of Islam say?"

These are very relevant questions, questions which any person who wants to understand Islam and Muslims is entitled to
have answered in an honest and straight-forward manner. It is
readily apparent that Islam—or any other religion can be effective in people's lives only to the extent that they practice it. And

there are as many kinds of Muslims in the world today as there are followers of any other religion. As there are Jews and Christians and Hindus and Buddhists who are totally committed to their faiths and others who are nominal followers the "Sunday" or "Christmas-and-Easter Christians," or less than that so there are Muslims of varying degrees of conviction and practice of Islam. On forms and applications, in the space where one is asked to state his religion, all of these alike write the name of the faith into which they were born, but this is merely a cold and meaningless statistic which says nothing at all about their degree of understanding, conviction and commitment to their faith.

The answers to these questions are inextricably connected with the present situation of the Muslim world, and in the section which follows we will attempt, in the briefest possible form, to give some idea concerning this very complex subject. The point to be borne in mind is that the Muslims who come from it to America or other countries of the West are the Muslim world in miniature; one can find representatives of its types in every shade and degree. If all, or even most, Muslims were true in word and deed to the religion which they profess, there would be no need to write these lines. Everyone is aware of the extreme greed, materialism,decadence and un-Islamic behavior of some of the newly-rich Arabs, of the total lack of Islamic values and behavior of many other "Muslims" from various parts of the East, and some people find it revolting. If these are Muslims, one may ask, what kind of religion is Islam?

Yes, it is undoubtedly true that all these people call themselves Muslims, or at least that is what they say when asked what faith they profess. But if the reader has ever met a true Muslim, whether he or she is an Arab or a Pakistani or Turk or African or Indonesian or European or American or whatever it may be, he will certainly be aware of the difference between a Muslim by name and a Muslim by conviction, commitment and life. Yet even such sincere and committed Muslims sometimes do wrong or act out of character. And then that is also not Islam.

For Islam is a complete and perfect system of life revealed by Almighty God and exemplified in the life of His messenger,

Muhammad (peace be on him), the totality of all the concepts, attitudes, values, moral guidelines, behaviors, worships and living patterns we have been talking about in these pages and much, much more. It remains so just as much today as when it was first proclaimed on earth, its validity and truth totally independent of whether Muslims practice it faithfully or fail to practice it, now or in the past or in the future. It is therefore essential to maintain a clear distinction in our minds between what Islam is and what Muslims are, between the religion itself and the people who profess it, and if the behavior which we observe among Muslims does not correctly reflect Islam, to draw our conclusions concerning the individual Muslims themselves rather than concerning the religion which they profess but do not necessarily practice in a faithful and conscientious manner.

VI.
ISLAM AND THE MUSLIM WORLD

In order to understand what is happening to Muslims, it is necessary to have a look at what is happening to the Muslim world. During the past century-and-a-half, the entire world has gone through tremendous upheavals, particularly in the realm of religion and values. While Europe and America were experiencing a profound loss of belief in religion, due in part to the irreconcilable conflict between science and what was supposed to be the "revealed Word" and in part to changes in people's values and outlooks as a result of massive changes in technology and patterns of living, the Muslim world too was experiencing a great crisis in the realm of religion and values.

During this period, due to a complex interplay of forces, while the hold of Christianity was weakening in the West, the influence of Islam was also becoming attenuated in the East. As a result, many Muslims so far lost sight of the true reality of their faith that masses of them took the traditions of their societies, some of which were from Islam and others from sources other than Islam, to be Islam itself. Their understanding of Islam as a dynamic, revolutionary system of life shrank until all that remained to them of it was a set of confused, quasi-Islamic traditions, some faded remnants of Islamic values and behavior, and perhaps (but often not even that) praying and fasting in Ramadan, reading the Quran when someone died, and celebrating the Festivals. Others went to the opposite extreme, placing great emphasis on the worship aspects of Islam while ignoring all the rest of its teachings, especially in the area of striving, seeking knowledge, developing resources, political responsibility, cleanliness, etc. Muslim children living in areas outside the Arab world learned from pious but often ignorant teachers to pronounce the words of the Quran without understanding anything of their meaning, much less living by them, while in other places, youngsters grew up still more ignorant of Islam, believing it to be something related to the older generation which one is supposed to respect but which has no relevance or place in contemporary life.

At the same time, the Western influence emerged in the Muslim world and little by little grew stronger and stronger. In the past this trend was fueled by Western imperialism and the presence of Western officials, as well as by Christian missionaries and westernized, often Western-educated, natives who had returned home from a sojourn in Europe or America. Later industrial and commercial interests, finding a ready market for Western goods and expertise in Muslim countries, enthusiastically accelerated the process. Muslims became uneasily conscious of their own material backwardness and lack of modernity in comparison with the West, assisted by contact with Western goods and the lure of its life-styles, conveyed to every part of the globe by Western movies, media and propaganda. The West was seen as a glamorous utopia, and adoption of some of the trappings of its culture was looked upon as the instant way to modernization and progress.

Unfortunately, what was adopted were not the outstanding and excellent aspects of Western culture but only the most superficial and harmful ones, which were simultaneously applauded by many onlookers in the West as obvious signs that the Muslim world was now beginning to wake up and come of age: the old equation of bars, boogie and bikinis with progress and modernity. Under the impact of all this, many Muslims accepted Western society's dictum that religion, moral values and the pursuit of meaning be given no serious emphasis or importance in society. Its criteria of being civilized material advancement and the discarding of traditional values were accepted by them as the true measure of the greatness of a society without their grasping the essential fact that genuine civilization must rest on a firm base of sound spiritual and moral principles, lacking which material progress simply becomes de-civilizing, de-humanizing and destructive.

Consequently the present era has seen the emergence of three basic types of Muslims, who have their counterparts in other faiths as well. One is the individual for whom Islam is merely a vague tradition which more often than not he prefers to have nothing to do with, who inscribes himself "Muslim" on his passport simply because he is not a Christian or a Buddhist or anything else. He may either profess some outward tokens of respect for Islam or may reject it totally, but in any case it does not occur to him to guide his life by it or to try to practice it faithfully, and he regards those who do so as backward and stupid.

This is understandable enough in view of the fact that almost invariably such individuals lack knowledge and understanding of Islam as a total world-view and system of life; moreover, they may never have been close to or even known anyone who could provide an example of real understanding and commitment to Islam. Such a "Muslim" may never have prayed in his life and may not even know how since he was not taught. For him Islam is simply a relic of ancient history. He may feel an occasional twinge of pride in his Islamic heritage when it is mentioned and may even come to the "defense" of Islam when it is attacked. Or he may think about it once in a while when someone dies ("Where am I going to go when this happens to me? Oh, well, God is merciful"), but he is too preoccupied with his daily activities and with his family and possessions and pleasures to follow up this train of thought. Many social problems and vices have by now crept into the lives of such Muslims, including an increasing incidence of divorce, sexual license, alcoholism, and total loss of values and direction. Basically they are Muslims-by-name, no different either in their concepts or behavior from people who have no religion and no values, for in fact they hate neither, and they are often very hostile to Islam and to Muslims who adhere to it faithfully.

The second group are the traditional Muslims. They may

understand the basic concepts of Islam, may have some degree of Islamic knowledge and may follow the Islamic teachings to some extent but they do not understand it as a complete and dynamic system for all aspects of the human being's life nor do they adhere to its requirements in all aspects of their lives consistently and as a matter of principle and obligation. In their minds Islam is often intermixed with many pseudo-lslamic practices common to their societies, many of which are completely contrary to the Islamic teachings although they have acquired some sort of an "Islamic" sanction or flavor, and with many westernized ways of thought and behavior as well. They definitely believe in God and Islam, but in a theoretical sort of way which does not carry enough conviction to move them steadily and consistently toward a totally Islamic orientation and way of life. Because they do not conceive of Islam as a complete system for all aspects of life, they are often critical of or look down on those who do as having "gone too far" in the matter of religion.

The third group consists of those Muslims who understand the religion they profess as a total system and who have consciously decided to pattern their lives according to it. Their world-view and frame of reference is that of Islam, their obedience, loyalty and devotion are for God alone; their goal is the hereafter: and their community is the community of believers. Many among this group are highly educated individuals who have arrived at such a position as a result of reflection on what is happening in the world around them. They are a unique group, part of the small yet strong company of true believers in God who have been lining in submission to Him since the first prophet, Adam (peace be on him), walked on earth, in obedience to His guidance.

Without question, to reach such a level of Islamic commitment requires an understanding which, due to very faulty and inadequate approaches to Islamic education even in "Muslim" countries, few are able to attain. Moreover, the appeal of westernization and modernity is so strong that few people in the Muslim world hate yet grasped the fact that material advancement is not necessarily the road to either true self-respect or satisfaction, and that it has not brought real happiness and well-being to the peoples of the West but instead a staggering array of societal and environmental problems because it has been divorced from the spiritual and moral dimensions which are as integral and essential a part of the human being's nature as is his material aspect.

When we survey the Muslim world today use see a confused and troubled picture in which political instability plays a major role. In spite of the Islamic requirement of a leader elected from among the people who consults with them in the conduct of affairs in very few countries of the Muslim world today are the governments elected by the people and responsive to their needs, or capable of providing leadership and stability to their countries: rather there are, by and large, the rulers and the ruled. And although in most cases they professed Islam and often made a public show of piety, among the rulers of the Muslim world in recent years have been many who were dictators and oppressors of the most vicious sort. They stifled all criticism and dissent in their societies, whether by individuals, groups or the press, by sadistically oppressive means, making ruthless use of highly-trained secret police and intelligence services to suppress anyone they considered a threat to their unbridled power; they filled the prisons of their "Muslim" countries to overflowing with tens of thousands of sincere and committed Muslims, many belonging to the intelligentsia, who were trying to call for a revival of Islam in their societies or to question the policies or actions of the ruler. Hair-raising nazi-style tortures were applied to countless numbers of them under which many died, and some of the best among them were executed for fabricated "crimes" in order to silence the voice of truth so the ruler might continue unimpeded in his relentless drive for absolute power.

Country after country in the Muslim world has seen rulers of this kind during the past half century or more, men who, although often Muslims themselves, hated and feared the very name of Islam because it constituted the only real challenge to their unchecked power and ambition, and who threw all their energies into trying to suppress it by oppressing Muslims. The Islamic requirement and demand of the people themselves for basic human freedoms, social justice and good rule were systematically and ruthlessly stifled. Any incident occurring under such conditions was blamed on Islam and "Muslim fanaticism," as if one had to be either a Muslim or a fanatic to want freedom and justice: indeed incidents expressly manufactured by the government for the purpose of discrediting Muslims have not been unknown. But since Islam, which is deep within the lifeblood of Muslims even though they may be indifferent to its requirements, could not be so easily dismissed such rulers attempted to reduce It to mere piety and acts of worship lest it emerge as strong, dynamic movement in which each individual feels a keen sense of responsibility for how the country is governed. What happens to its resources which belong to all the people the morals and behavior of its officials, and the entire host of matters over which governments have jurisdictions, which Almighty God has made the concern of every Muslim individual as a member of his society as well.

And what of the people in the face of all this while Muslims of the first type are busy living the life of the world, preoccupied with their possessions, enjoyments relationships and the increase of their material advantages the second type of Muslims live in some halfway house between total loss of Islamic values anal adherence to them. With various excuses and apologies for their lack of commitment. The Muslims in the third category stand firm on the Islamic principles and values, serving as a counter-balancing force against random progress and indiscriminate adoption of values and behaviors which are not appropriate for Muslims and can do great harm to their societies. Because of their certain and unwavering conviction of the truth of Islam, such individuals cannot be swayed in the direction of ideologies such as communism as can others due to their basic lack of convictions, especially in the face of the multitude of economic, political and social problems facing their countries at the present time.

Today, in spite of all these difficult circumstances, a wave of Islamic consciousness and pride is being felt throughout the

Muslim world. For many years the people of this area had been told in so many explicit and implicit ways that they were backward and inferior and that the only way to rise out of this state was to discard their religion and traditions and adopt westernization; many believed this and are now following the path of crass materialism. Others, having taken a good look at Western society, have become aware of its pitfalls and have grasped the fact that material progress and prosperity do not constitute the total fulfillment of the human being's nature nor provide him with the paradise on earth which they seemed to promise. After one attains all that, they ask, then what? Prosperity can leave an individual as inwardly empty as poverty. Such people have come to the realization that human beings must, by the necessity of their human nature, concern themselves with something much more significant than merely the material sphere, with meaning and not simply with matter. As a result of all this, they have come to a deep and unshakable conviction that whatever is most precious, whatever is most essential to the human being's existence, is to be found in their fourteen-hundred-year-old Islamic heritage, in their religion and its way of life rather than in any other system or ideology.

With this has also come the clear realization that the problems facing the Muslim world today are, very logically and directly, the result of Muslims falling away from Islam and that they can be solved only by a sincere and whole-hearted return to it: among the social, political and economic principles of Islam, principles which are compatible not with the present savage, opportunistic dog-eat-dog ethics of self-interest but with the highest and noblest values of human civilization, are to be found solutions for its complex ailments. Of all the trends evident in the Muslim world today materialism, nationalism. socialism. communism and Islam only Islam holds the certain promise, if applied with sincerity and intelligence, of bringing the peoples of this region, who have lived through so many serious upheavals both internal and external in recent years, into a state of stability and peace.

In a broader context than that of conditions in the Middle East today, we may remark that communism, materialism and all other ideologies which deny or give insignificant value to the human being's spiritual nature or concentrate on one aspect of his nature at the expense of the others must ultimately be viewed as the human being's futile attempts, by means of his very limited human perspective, to understand himself and find the right direction. Since early in the human being's career on this planet, various religions, philosophies, and systems of life and thought, including those which are dominant today, have crossed the stage of history and played their role. A look at the legacy of this history and at current trends in the world makes it clear that none of these has succeeded in resolving the essential conflicts and dilemmas within the human personality, for all of them have, in one form or another, either ignored vital aspects of the human being's relationship with Reality or given prominence to one aspect of life or of the human being's nature at the expense of others, creating frightening disharmonies and imbalances within human individuals and their societies which have, in the present era, come close to destroying humanity altogether.

In the midst of all this, Islam remains the one system the world has known which views the human being in a correct perspective within the context of total Reality and with a correct understanding of his true nature, providing a just balance between his material and spiritual aspects, between the human being's worldly aspirations and needs and his eternal goal. It is the only system which submits the human being and his life in its entirety to the One Who gives him that life and Who alone can be worthy of his submission, liberating him from the darkness of enslavement to man-made values, systems and desires into the light of servanthood to God, his true Master, alone. The truth of this is being realized with compelling certainty by more and more people in the East those who were born into Muslim families but who have now become conscious, steadfast Muslims by conviction and commitment and by many in the West as well. The grandeur and nobility of Islam is no longer an unknown, hidden thing, kept from the knowledge of the peoples of the West by lack of contact, prejudice or cultural differences difficult to surmount. More and more are joining the fold of Islam each day, realizing that it offers them that truth and that way of life for which they had been searching fruitlessly, perhaps for years, in other and often totally contradictory directions. To many, Islam is increasingly thought to be the wave of the future, the long misplaced legacy of the whole of humanity! not merely of people in lands where Islam has long been established, from its Lord, the God of the heavens and the earth, which holds out the promise to mankind, if applied with dedication and sincerity, of setting its feet upon the path of stability and balance, and bringing about such a total transformation in the human being's individual and collective existence as no man-made system, no obedience to gods of the human being's own invention, can ever succeed in doing.

PART FOUR:
THE ISLAMIC
WAY OF LIFE

VII.
THE PERFORMANCE OF THE ACTS OF WORSHIP

The first obligation of a Muslim, no matter where in the world he or she may happen to live, is to establish the acts of worship on a regular basis in his or her household. This means to observe *salah* regularly five times a day at the proper times, as well as the obligatory congregational Friday prayer; to fast throughout the month of Ramadan together with observing other recommended devotional practices; to pay *zakah* once a year if one has savings or property on which *zakah* is to be assessed; and to perform the *hajj* once in a lifetime if one has the means for the journey and for the support of one's dependents, and there is safety of travel to and from Arabia.

Let us now proceed to see how Muslims go about performing these worships in practical terms. *Hajj* has not been included in the discussion since it is, as a rule, a once-in-a-lifetime experience which we have already covered in detail in the preceding section.

PRAYER (*SALAH*)

The practice of regular *salah* is the most fundamental requirement in Islam, without which a Muslim is not fulfilling even his most basic obligation to God and may well have lost the most important and precious thing in his life, his perspective and sense of relatedness to his Creator. The *salah*

itself is prescribed in the Quran and the manner in which it is performed comes to us from the *sunnah* of Prophet Muhammad
(peace be on him). Hence all the Muslims of today, no matter
where in the world they may be, perform their *salah* in just the
same manner as did the Prophet of Islam some fourteen hundred
years ago. Consequently a Muslim from America can go to
Tunisia or Yugoslavia or Japan or India or Iraq or South Africa or
the Philippines or China, join congregational *salah*, and without
the least difficulty perform his worship just as he had been used
to doing in America because everyone else will also be performing it in the same way.

Salah can be performed almost anywhere in a mosque, a
home, one's place of work, outdoors or in any other clean place
either individually or in congregation. Congregational *salah*
(consisting of two or more worshippers, one of whom leads the
prayer) is preferable to individual *salah* because of its obvious
aspects of brotherhood and solidarity. In the Muslim world
mosques are the established places for congregational worship.
Women as well as men may pray in mosques if they desire, but
it is preferable and customary that women pray in the privacy of
their homes, especially since leaving the home and children to go
to the mosque five times a day is neither practical nor possible
for most women; many mosques have separate sections for
women in order that they may pray in complete privacy and so
there may be no distraction due to physical mingling between
men and women.

So great is the importance of *salah* in keeping the Muslim
strong and steadfast in Islam that it is an obligation under all circumstances, even when one is ill, traveling, or in battle.
However, certain concessions have been made for such situations. Thus, one who is ill and cannot perform *salah* in the usual
manner may pray sitting in a chair or lying in bed, moving his
hands (or if this is not possible only his eyes) to indicate the various motions. When one is traveling, he can shorten his *salah* and
combine the second and third, and the fourth and fifth prescribed
prayers of the day so that he prays three times a day instead of
five; he can, if necessary, pray while seated in his vehicle or
mount and similar concessions are made for soldiers in battle. If

salah is not performed at the proper time for any reason, it is to be made up as soon as possible thereafter: it may not be missed altogether. The sole exception to this is women during menstruation and up to forty days following childbirth: they are excused from *salah* entirely for the duration of their condition for the reason that prescribed purity (that is, the absence of bodily discharges) is a requisite for the performance of *salah*.

Salah is preceded by an ablution known as *wudu* during which the exposed parts of the body are washed: this brief preparation of the mind and body for the act of prayer is an essential requirement. If water is not available (during travel or under other unusual conditions) or if its use is likely to injure the worshiper (as in the case of serious illness or wounds), he may instead make a symbolic cleansing called *tayammum* without the use of water. The ablution maybe maintained from one prayer to another if it is not broken by any bodily discharge, such as urination or defecation, passing gas, seminal discharge, vomiting, bleeding or sleeping, etc. A full bath by means of running water (*ghusl*) is required after marital relations, seminal emission. and the termination of menstruation or postpartum bleeding. The five prayers are observed during the following time periods:

(1) Dawn (*salah al-fajr*) from the first light of dawn until shortly before sunrise.

(2) Noon (*salah adh-dhuhr*) from just past high noon until mid-afternoon.

(3) Afternoon (*salah al-asr*) from mid-afternoon until shortly before sunset.

(4) Evening (*salah al-maghrib*) from just past sunset until the last light fades.

(5) Night (*salah al-isha*) from dark until shortly before dawn.

After performing ablution, the Muslim prepares for his *salah* by determining the direction of Mecca (the *qiblah*) and facing it. For the sake of cleanliness, since his forehead and clothing will touch the floor or ground during prayer, he removes his shoes (except on occasion while traveling and spreads out some sort of a clean covering. often a small rug). Men may not pray in a garment which does not cover them, at minimum, from the navel to the knee and women are required to be entirely covered with a loose, concealing garment which leaves only the face and hands exposed. *Salah* consists of a combination of words and move- ments performed in units known as *rak'at*s or cycles. The wor- shippers begins his *salah* by standing at attention raising his hands to the side of his head and pronouncing the words "Allahu *Akbar*" (God is Greater). This utterance constitutes a declaration that he is now in the presence of God and consecrated to His wor- ship. This phrase is repeated again and again with each change of posture throughout the prayer.

In the first cycle the worshipper standing quietly at attention, recites the opening verses of the Quran, *Surat al-Fateha*, fol- lowed be another Quranic passage of his choosing. After this he bows with his hands on his knees as one who is ready to receive his Master's orders, while he whispers words of glorification of God. After briefly standing erect for a moment, he prostrates himself on the floor or ground in a gesture of total submission and humility before God while he silently repeats words of glo- rification. This is followed by the second cycle performed in an identical manner. After every two cycles the worshipper sits briefly, praising God, invoking His peace on the Prophet, on him- self and on all righteous people, and repeating the declaration of faith. The remaining cycles are identical except that they contain only one recitation from the Quran (that of the opening verses (*surat al-fateha*) instead of two. The final cycle is followed by the same prayer said in a sitting posture, together with a suppli- cation for God's blessings on the Prophet and his people, and then the *salah* finishes with the greeting of peace, "*Assalamu alaikum wa rahmatallah*" (peace be on you, and God's mercy). The worshipper may then remain sitting to offer his own person- al supplications and glorification of God, either using the prayers of the Prophet or his own words and language .

A fixed number of cycles in each prayer are obligatory (*fard*), while others are recommended (*sunnah*, that is, following the Prophet's practice). Thus, while it is permissible to pray only a minimum number of cycles, it is preferable to add to them the number of additional cycles which the Prophet used to pray and recommended, and if one wishes he may offer still additional cycles, again in keeping with the Prophet's own practice.

Congregational prayers are performed in just the same sequence and detail. In Muslim countries congregational prayers are observed five times a day in every mosque, the time of the prayer announced by the call to prayer (*adhan*) broadcast from the mosque, usually via microphone. *Imams* (leaders of the *salah*), whose salary is paid by the government, are appointed in many mosques; otherwise the worshippers select a man of learning and piety from among their number each time they gather to pray. The *imam* stands in front of the congregation, the worshippers lined up in straight, orderly rows shoulder to shoulder, and leads them in worship; they follow his movements in unison and absolute discipline, expressive of the unity of Muslims as one brotherhood submitting to the One God, following one Prophet, and obedient to the leadership of a single *imam* appointed from among them.

Islam also establishes a weekly congregational worship on Friday (*salah al-jumah*) which is observed around noon in the major mosques of a city, taking the place of the noon prayer for those who attend it. This Friday worship is obligatory for Muslim men. While the Friday worship is not obligatory for women, they may attend it if they wish and find it convenient; otherwise they pray the noon prayer at home as usual. The Friday worship consists of a sermon concerning any matter related to Islam or the life of Muslims, followed by two cycles of *salah*. The function of the sermon is to educate Muslims in matters pertaining to their faith, recall them to the observance of its teachings, and inform them of current events of mutual concern. Although in most Muslim countries Friday is a holiday rather than Sunday, Friday has not been prescribed as a day of rest but rather of obligatory worship, and work and business transactions are permitted as usual before and after the time of the Friday prayer.

There are a number of other forms of non-regular *salah* which Muslims perform on various occasions. The more common ones are the nightly *taraweeh* prayer during Ramadan; funeral *salah*, always performed in congregation; the *salah* of the two festivals; *tahajjud*, the *salah* offered during the last one third of the night, which is especially dear to those Muslims who want to increase in nearness to God by performing additional devotions; and *istikhara*, a *salah* consisting of two cycles followed by an appropriate supplication, to be performed when one is faced with a difficult decision about which he seeks guidance from God.

The Muslim child who is born into a household where *salah* is a natural part of the daily routine becomes accustomed to it from an early age. He sees his parents and others praying and joins in occasionally in his baby's fashion when he is still a toddler. Because *salah* is to have pleasurable associations in a child's mind, Muslim children are permitted to move among the worshippers without hindrance, following the example of the Prophet (peace be on him) who used to hold his grandsons on his shoulders while he prayed. A very young child can learn passages from the Quran in Arabic just as easily as he might memorize nursery rhymes, even if Arabic is not his native language, and as soon as he is old enough he can learn their meanings as well. By the time they are seven years old, children are supposed to be praying all the prayers, even though they may have to be reminded again and again, and by the age of ten *salah* five times a day becomes obligatory. Thus the Muslim child grows into the regular performance of *salah* easily and naturally, step by step, as the means by which he expresses his deep love and thankfulness to God, not only in words but with his entire being.

Salah is the central point of the Muslim's existence, without which he would not be able to maintain a strong and vital link with his Lord or continue his unremitting inner struggle against temptation and wrong-doing. Thus, no matter where on earth he may be, it is at once his duty and a necessity of his being to maintain *salah* faithfully and, whenever possible, in the company of his fellow-Muslims. Hence, while many Muslims living in the Western world may not have access to mosques, in many communities congregational prayers, especially that of Friday, are observed regularly in some designated place such as a university facility, an Islamic center, or someone's home.

FASTING (SAWM)

The month of Ramadan is a period of special religious significance and activity during which Muslims fast each day as a means of learning discipline, self-restraint and flexibility on the material level, the prescribed fast of Ramadan involves total abstinence from all food, drink, tobacco and marital intercourse during the daylight hours, and on the behavioral level, abstinence from falsehood, speaking ill of others, quarreling or engaging in angry talk, discussion of disreputable matters, and wrong behavior of any sort.

In addition to this, throughout Ramadan especially intensive devotional activities are carried on, both individually and collectively. It is *sunnah* to complete the reading or recitation of the Holy Quran during this month. *Taraweeh salah* is performed every night after the final prayer of the day, either individually or in congregation; it consists of between eight and twenty cycles, performed in sets of two cycles each. During the final ten days of Ramadan, many Muslims throughout the world observe retreat in mosques, spending the time in prayer and reading the Quran, and during this period the Night of Power, which will be discussed in the next section, is also commemorated.

The keynote to all the observances of Ramadan is self-discipline and self-control. Although in some Muslim countries the work schedule is modified during this month, in many places Muslims must carry on with their work and other activities even though they may be hungry, thirsty and tired. Fasting is in no sense an excuse for neglect of work or obligations, idleness, irritability or outbursts of temper, but, on the contrary, should be a total inner state leading to patience and self-control.

Although fasting does not become obligatory on Muslim youngsters until they reach puberty many children have had some practice at fasting long before they reach that age. A special atmosphere prevails in Muslim countries throughout Ramadan. As a rule, even those Muslims who do not observe the *salah* or other Islamic obligations, fast during this month, for fasting in Ramadan is a community-wide observance with social as well as spiritual aspects. In spite of the apparent hardship of fasting, Ramadan is a very enjoyable period, especially in the Muslim world to which people look forward year after year. And when the Festival of Ending the Fast, comes at the conclusion of the month, it is a wonderful and happy occasion for all Muslims, especially for the children.

Let us now take a look at the basic rules of fasting. Actually they are quite simple. First of all, every day of Ramadan is a day of fasting.[37] Fasting is obligatory on all Muslims past puberty, with the following exceptions: sick persons to whom fasting is likely to be injurious, persons who are traveling for whom fasting involves hardship, women during menstruation and up to forty days following childbirth, pregnant women and nursing mothers if fasting is likely to harm the mother or infant, the very old, and the insane.

The latter two categories are permanently exempt from fasting, while the others are exempt only for the duration of their conditions and must make up the missed fasts at any time before the beginning of the next Ramadan if possible. If one has a permanent condition which makes fasting impossible or dangerous to health, he is permitted instead to give to a needy person a sum equivalent to one meal for each day he did not fast. If a Muslim is not fasting on any day of Ramadan for any of the above-mentioned reasons, he is not to eat or drink in front of others who are fasting out of courtesy and in order not to undermine them.

The period of fasting begins each morning of Ramadan about ten minutes before the first light of dawn becomes visible and lasts until sunset. A declaration of intention to fast a silent statement in any words or language that one intends to fast today for the sake of God must he made at some time before noon. It is *sunnah* to break the fast immediately after the sun has set after which the evening prayer is performed and to have a meal before dawn at which time the next day's fast begins and of course the dawn prayer is observed at dawn as usual.

The practice of breaking the fast at sunset and getting up to eat before dawn is a special characteristic of Islamic fasting. In Islam fasting is not an ascetic or self-mortifying practice but an act of self-discipline and obedience to God. Obedience includes strictly carrying out His order to begin fasting before dawn and break the fast exactly at sunset.

Voluntary fasting outside Ramadan follows the same rules as the fasting of Ramadan. However. it should not be continuous. day-after-day fasting, apart from a few specific days during the year on which the Prophet himself (peace be on him) practiced fasting and recommended it. Again, although marital intercourse is prohibited during the hours of fasting, it is permissible during the night hours, once more making it clear that this refraining from meeting otherwise lawful needs during the daylight hours is intended as a means of self-discipline, not as an ascetic practice which Islam dislikes.

It should be noted that because Islam uses a lunar rather than a solar calendar, any given date falls ten days earlier each year (eleven days in a leap year) than in the preceding one. Consequently Ramadan (and all other dates) rotates throughout the seasons, completing the cycle of twelve months in about thirty-three years. Hence Ramadan sometimes falls in summer, sometimes in winter, and sometimes in between in the various parts of the world; people living in every clime experience it, therefore, during all the seasons. Fasting is naturally quite easy during the short days of winter, but can be extremely taxing in the heat of tropical summers. Under such conditions the fasting Muslim learns that food and drink are indeed precious gifts from his Lord, to be accepted with thankfulness and not taken for granted. He also learns to feel with the poor who frequently experience the same state of hunger he is tasting during this month, and thus his hands are especially open in charity during Ramadan.

Although Muslims living in the West can as a rule carry out all their religious obligations during Ramadan without difficulty, they invariably miss the special atmosphere and activities which are common in the Muslim world during this month. Hence they often try to compensate for the lack of these by inviting other Muslims for the evening meal and by community-wide observances such as frequent gatherings for the evening meal as well as congregational *taraweeh* prayers.

POOR-DUE

In practical terms, the poor-due (*zakah*) is the sum of money which is to be paid on various categories of property which is to be used to assist the poor of the community, or for the welfare of Muslims and the propagation of Islam. *Zakah* is assessed on money or possessions only after a year has passed since its accumulation and it is calculated and paid once a year according to well-established rules. Since it is the duty of the Muslim state to collect and distribute *zakah*, what do Muslims living in non-Muslim countries do with their *zakah* payments? There are a number of alternatives.

Zakah can be paid directly, in such a way that it does not hurt feelings, to needy, deserving Muslims in one's own community; it can be sent to Islamic organizations or centers in one's country of residence to be distributed at their discretion; or it can be sent to individuals or organizations in the Muslim world for distribution.

VIII.
ISLAMIC FESTIVALS AND OBSERVANCES

The pre-Islamic Arabs of Mecca observed numerous festivals which revolved around their polytheistic religion. After the advent of Islam, the Holy Prophet (peace be on him) abolished all these. In their place Muslims were given two major feasts, the festival marking the end of the month of fasting (*eid al-fitr*) and the festival marking the Prophet Abraham's sacrifice (*eid al-adha*), the celebration of which, with the worship of God and with joy and happiness, is a religious obligation for Muslims. We will discuss these in more detail presently.

In addition to these two festivals, as we have already mentioned, Muslims observe the Night of Power (*lailat al-qadr*), the night on which the first revelation of the Holy Quran came to Prophet Muhammad (may God's peace and blessings be on him). Although its exact date is not known with certainty, it falls during one of the odd numbered nights during the last ten days of Ramadan. On this night, according to the Prophet's *hadith*, the doors of God's mercy and forgiveness are open to all who call upon Him. The night during which it is commemorated, usually the night preceding the twenty-seventh day of Ramadan, is observed by devout Muslims by the performance of *taraweeh salah*, night-long devotions, recitations of the Quran and acts of charity.

The first day of the month of Muharram is the first day of the Islamic year. It marks the date of the Prophet's migration (*hijrah*) from Mecca to Medina, which constitutes the most important date for Islam because it signalzed the real beginning of the Islamic community and system. In Mecca the Muslims had been cruelly persecuted, unable either to preach or to practice Islam openly. After the Prophet and his Companions migrated to Medina, joining themselves with the Medinite Muslims to form a single united community, they were able to establish an Islamic society and state practicing Islam fully and completely, with the Prophet (peace be on him) as their leader, spiritual guide and head of state. This is why Muharram rather than the Prophet's birthday or the Night of Power constitutes the Islamic New Year. Although this occasion is observed by some Muslims by an exchange of greetings and sweet dishes, its observance is a purely traditional rather than Islamic occasion.

Some Muslims also celebrate the birth date of the Prophet (peace be on him); however, this observance is not based either on the Quran, the Prophet's *sunnah* or the practice of his Companions because Islam is not a religion centering on any human being,[38] the celebration of the Prophet's birthday is not a part of the religion but is a purely traditional observance, which is marked by gatherings or radio and television programs to recall the Prophet's life and mission, calling on Muslims to renew their commitment to follow his example. We now turn our attention to the two major Islamic festivals.

THE FESTIVAL ENDING THE FAST

Eid al-fitr, the festival which marks the end of Ramadan, occurs on the first of the lunar month of Shawwal, and its celebration extends over a period of three days. This occasion is a time of great joy and thankfulness for Muslims because they have completed their obligation of fasting a month-long discipline of the the body and appetites and it is an occasion for celebration. The festival is characterized by a special *salah*, visiting and exchanging greetings and good wishes and it is a time of special happiness for the children.

A few days before the time of the festival *salah*, which is held in the morning, usually shortly after sunrise, a special obligatory charity must be given. This is a specified amount of grain or other foodstuff or alternatively a sum of money equivalent to the cost of one meal to be given on behalf of every member of one's family to needy Muslims, either directly or through some Islamic organization. The festival prayer is a special additional congregational prayer which is *sunnah* (practiced and recommended by the prophet) rather than obligatory. Traditionally in Muslim countries every able-bodied male attends; the Prophet also urged that all women should be present even if they were not able to pray due to their monthly indisposition. This prayer is held either in the largest mosques of a city or in an open area where many thousands of people can gather. It consists of two cycles with additional recitations "Allahu *Akbar*," followed by a sermon appropriate to the occasion.

Traditionally both the festivals are occasions for exchanging visits with relatives and friends throughout the entire period of observance of each festival. Gifts (usually of money or new clothes) are given to children, who delight in wearing their beautiful new things for the occasion, and special sweets or other foods are served to guests. Throughout the Muslim world, the atmosphere during the days of the festivals is distinctly special, combining social with spiritual aspects in a way which brings joy and pleasure to people of all ages and walks of life.

THE FESTIVAL OF SACRIFICE

This is the greater of the two major festivals, the period of its celebration extending over four days. This festival marks the annual completion of the *hajj*. It falls on the tenth of the month of Dhul-Hijjah approximately two-and-a-half months after the Festival Ending the Fast, rotating clockwise around the year and occurring ten days earlier annually, as do all dates.

At this time, those who have gone to *hajj* are completing their observances in Mina with the slaughter of an animal (although this is not a requirement for all pilgrims) and the termination of their state of *ihram*. At the same time, as part of their celebration of *eid al-adha*, countless Muslims throughout the world are sacrificing animals (this is *sunnah* rather than obligatory) in commemoration of Prophet Abraham's sacrifice of a sheep in the place of his son Ishmael, as commanded by God. The example of Prophet Abraham (peace be upon him) is recalled on this occasion as a model of total obedience and surrender to God for Muslims of all time to follow.

Then what happens to the slaughtered animal? Its meat is divided into three equal portions—one for the use of the family, one to be given to neighbors and friends, and one to be given away to the poor, to be used as food; the portions which are distributed are given away as meat (not cooked or prepared). This giving meat constitutes the special charity of this festival in the place of a monetary one, due to which *eid al-adha* is one time in the year—in many places perhaps the only time-when the poor may have meat to eat. Apart from these differences, the other aspects of the observance of this festival are identical to those of *eid al-fitr*.

How do Muslims living in the Western world celebrate these two festivals? *Eid* prayers are observed in every community where Muslims reside and gatherings to celebrate the occasions are common, for example, a community-wide dinner followed by a program with talks and suitable entertainment, a program or gifts for the children, etc. Many Muslim children stay home from school to celebrate these festivals, and in some areas the festivals are recognized by school authorities as holidays for Muslim youngsters. Although it may take a special effort to make the festivals a happy time, especially for the children, in an environment in which Muslims are often a very small number, this is a religious obligation for Muslims as well as a social one, wherever they may happen to reside.

IX.
FAMILY LIFE

Family life is one of the most important and emphasized areas in the Islamic system of life, and it is an aspect which remains very clear and strong among the vast majority of Muslims today. We will now have a look at the kinds of interrelationships Islam establishes between husband and wife, parents and children, and among other members of the family group.

MARRIAGE AND THE ROLES OF HUSBAND AND WIFE

Among Muslims the selection of a marriage partner is a very different process than in the Western world. Because Islam emphasizes chastity and modesty so strongly, there is very little contact between young men and young women in most parts of the Muslim world. Secondary schools are generally not co-educational, and, except among the very westernized, boys and girls do not mix, date, or, in particular engage in pre-marital intimacy of any kind. And while love is certainly considered very important in the Muslim marriage, for Muslim couples love as a rule comes after rather than before the marriage.

The selection of a marriage partner is therefore generally (but not necessarily) made by the parents, especially in the case of a girl. The young people concerned can express a preference, can state what they want in a prospective partner, and can take an active role in the ultimate selection but ordinarily they do not go out and try to find a spouse on their own. Either the boy's or the girl's family may initiate a proposal but in practice it is customarily the boy who does the asking. This is done either through contact between his parents, other relatives or close friends with the parents of the girl; without her consent and approval of her father or guardian, who gives her away, marriage cannot take place. Depending on the traditions of the particular society in which they live, the prospective partners may or may not see each other before marriage, although Islam does give them this right. However, if they do meet at any time prior to marriage, this is always to be in the presence of other people since Islam forbids a Muslim man and woman who are not related to each other either by marriage or a *mahram* relationship to be alone with one another.[39]

In Islam marriage is not a sacrament but rather a legal, binding contract between a man and a woman which establishes the licitness, permanence and responsibleness of their relationship, an acceptance of one another as spouses with a mutual commitment to live together according to the teachings of Islam. Both are to be mindful of their duty to God and their responsibilities to one another in all aspects of their interaction.

> *"O mankind, be careful of your duty to your Lord, Who created you from a single soul and from it created its mate, and from the two of them spread abroad a multitude of men and women. Be careful of your duty to God in Whom you claim (your rights) of one another, and toward the wombs.*[40] *Verily, God is Watcher over you."* (4:1)

As we have seen, Islam assigns the leadership of the family to men, for in general they have been endowed with somewhat greater physical and emotional strength and endurance than women. For this reason they have also been made responsible for supporting and maintaining women—not only their wives and daughters but also female relatives who may be in need of help and support.

"Men are responsible for women because God has given the one more than the other, and because they spend of their property (for the support of women). Virtuous women are therefore obedient, guarding in their (husbands') absence that which God has guarded." (4:34)[41]

The wife is her husband's companion and helpmate, who is, together with him, responsible for the affairs of the household, the physical and emotional well-being of its members, and the training of the children. She should obey her husband unless he asks her to disobey God in which case she must not obey him, and for his part he should be considerate and concerned for her welfare. As the above Quranic verse indicates, she is also responsible for the proper management of her husband's possessions and property, for the guarding of his honor, dignity and respectability, and for reserving her sexuality exclusively for the man she has married.

In Islam a woman, married or single, is seen as a person in her own right, not merely as an adjunct to her husband. Thus, for example, she has the full right of ownership and disposal of her own property and earnings even after marriage, and when she marries she retains her own family name instead of taking that of her husband. The Western stereotype of the Muslim woman as a mere household drudge, preoccupied from morning to night with cooking, cleaning and looking after the children, with no spirituality, interests, personality or life of her own, who is debarred from contributing in a constructive manner to society has no basis in the Islamic teachings.[42] For Islam regards men and women as completely equal in terms of accountability to God and in possessing unique personalities of their own.[43] It prescribes for both the same religious obligations apart from the concessions made for women's reproductive cycle and makes conscious commitment to Islam the doing of good striving with all one's efforts in God's path the development of spirituality and seeking knowledge equally the duty of both men and women as the following Quranic verses indicate:

> *"And their Lord answered them 'Verily, I will not allow the work of any worker male or female to be lost. You proceed from one another.'"* (3:195)

> *"And whoever does good whether male or female and he (or she) is a believer these will enter paradise and they will not be wronged by so much as the groove of a date stone."* (4:194)

> *"And the believers—men and women—are protecting friends to one another. They enjoin what is right and forbid what is wrong they observe regular salah and pay zakah, and they obey God and His Messenger. As for these, God will have mercy on them. Verily, God is Mighty. Wise. God promises the Believers, men and women, gardens underneath which rivers flow, to abide therein—blessed dwellings in gardens of Eden. And greater (than that), God's good pleasure: that is the supreme success."* (9:71-72)

At the same time, Islam recognizes that women have a more delicate, sensitive and emotional nature than men and men are asked to treat them in accordance with this nature. There are many beautiful *hadith* of the Prophet (peace be on him) which enjoin kindness and consideration for women and advise Muslims to treat their wives with respect, honor and that quality of tenderness which suits the delicacy of their feminine nature, the best men, he said, are those who are best to their wives.[44]

Because the natures of the male and the female are not the same, each has been entrusted with a particular role and function in society: these roles are complementary and each is equally basic and essential to the functioning of the society. Within this framework there is freedom for both men and women to pursue what is important to them and to contribute to society in keeping with their own individual skills and interests, provided their responsibilities for the home are not neglected and their work does not in any way jeopardize their dignity and modesty. Women must fill many essential positions in society which they can handle better or instead of men, for example, some branches of medicine, nursing, education, social work and other areas. In the Prophet's time we find women enduring persecution, exile and even martyrdom for the sake of their faith at the hands of the pagans together with men, and during battle carrying water to the wounded, tending the injured and on occasion participating in the fighting as well. We find them discussing and even disputing various matters with the Prophet himself, and on another occasion a woman standing up in the mosque to correct the caliph Umar on a legal point. We find Aisha, the Prophet's widows in later life an expert in Islamic jurisprudence, consulted by many eminent Muslims, while her sister Asma, as a young girl and again as an old woman of ninety, did great deeds of courage and heroism.

Concerning the marriage relationship God says:

> *"And among His signs is that He created mates from among yourselves that you may live in tranquillity with them, and He has put love and mercy between your hearts."* (30:21)

> *"It is He Who created you from a single soul, and from it created its mate that he might take rest in her . . . ."* (7:189)

The tone of marriage in Islam is thus one of mutual respect, kindness, love, companionship and harmonious interaction. In her husband the wife has a friend and partner to share her life and concerns, to cherish and protect her, and to help her bear responsibilities which would be very difficult or impossible for her to handle alone, while a man has in his wife a companion and helper who can give him peace, comfort and repose in his struggle with the rough-and-tumble of the world's life. In the beautiful language of the Quran,

> *"They (wives) are your garments and you (husbands) are their garments,"* (2:187)

serving for one another the same function as a cherished piece of clothing: to be a comfort, a protection, a security, that which serves and beautifies and warms and enfolds and covers and conceals what is private from the eyes of the world.

Although for the sake of convenience women generally do the domestic work of the house, this is not required of them by Islam. A husband should help his wife with the household work following the example of the Prophet (peace be on him), who used to assist his wives, mend his own clothes and participate in manual work. And while the mother is generally the primary means of training the children, Islam neither expects nor wants her to carry out this extremely important task alone. It is the joint responsibility of husband and wife to bring up their children properly, and although the greater part of the daily work with the children generally falls to the share of the wife, the husband is the principal authority figure in the home who is responsible not only for the welfare but also for the behavior of all members of the family. Together husband and wife must provide an Islamic atmosphere in their home and a consistent approach to training in which they reinforce and support one another.

The marriage relationship also involves another fundamental responsibility: the responsibility of both husband and wife to meet one another's sexual needs and at the same time not to seek elsewhere for the satisfaction of these needs. While marriage in Islam legitimizes the fulfillment of an otherwise prohibited desire, it also requires that husband and wife reserve their sexuality exclusively for each other. There is to be no "playing around" in a Muslim marriage; adultery is, as we have seen, not only one of the most serious sins but also, in Islamic law, a heinous crime. Moreover, the protection of women from anything which dishonors, degrades or in any way exploits their sexuality is considered extremely essential. Islam therefore lays down certain limits for both men and women so that sexual attraction and expression will be confined solely to the private relationship of husband and wife, and hence will not become a source of harm or disruption in the society. This topic will be discussed further under the heading of "Relations Between the Sexes."

Marriages among Muslims are, by and large, remarkably stable, especially in contrast to marriage in much of the Western world today. This is due to a number of factors. The first of these is that, unlike the Western marriage, in which premarital love and intimacy are considered indispensable, the basic ingredient of the Muslim marriage is a common set of values, principles and ways of living. Consequently a Muslim husband and wife, even if they come from different cultures and backgrounds, possess the same basic world view, frame of reference, and many similar attitudes and habits which serve to bind them together in a harmonious relationship. Second, even with all the problems and pressures existing today in Muslim societies, marital and family stability is encouraged and reinforced by various societal institutions. This is in marked contrast to many parts of the Western world in which the breakdown of marriages is assisted-one could even say made inevitable—by innumerable societal pressures which not only weaken the commitment of the partners to each other but also weaken the capacity of individuals to maintain a stable and permanent relationship with another human being. Third, Muslims are as a rule used to living with other people and are consequently skilled in adjusting themselves to various relationships; for this reason they tend in general to be somewhat tolerant and forbearing in their interaction with others, even when there are differences or friction of one sort or another.

Another reason may be that Muslim men and women are generally quite accepting of their masculine and feminine roles. Consequently, because the division of roles and responsibilities between husband and wife is as a rule clearly defined and acknowledged, many problems and friction are avoided. Again, Muslims are generally surrounded by a network of many relationships with relatives and friends. This gives each partner his or her own life apart from the spouse, with many other satisfying relationships, emotional outlets and sources of support. Hence neither husband nor wife is forced to depend on a single relationship for all their emotional satisfactions, thus putting an almost insupportable burden on one's partner and untenable strains on the marriage, for the variety of rewarding interactions with others makes life tolerable even if there are friction between the partners.

In summary, to the Muslim marriage is not seen as a Hollywood style romance but as a flesh-and-blood relationship between two very human individuals. In such a relationship strains and problems sometimes do arise. When they do, they are dealt with within the marriage relationship, assisted by the cushioning effect of the society, rather than by breaking up the marriage and the family unit, which is in the long run more difficult and damaging than accommodating and showing tolerance and patience, except in extreme cases, in which divorce is not only desirable but essential. Because of all these built-in safeguards, therefore, marriage among Muslims is basically a stable and viable institution.

PARENT-CHILD RELATIONS

Among Muslims children are very much loved and wanted, a precious gift and trust from God. Although contraception is not prohibited, many couples have large families by choice because they genuinely love and want several children, and couples who are childless by choice are almost unheard-of. Parenthood is regarded as desirable and rewarding, the fulfillment of a universal human urge which has its beginnings in a small child's instinctive love for babies and dolls. To the Muslim, his or her child is a precious treasure, a gift from God and the fondness of Muslims of all nationalities for children is well known.

In particular the Muslim woman's role as mother is regarded as being of the highest importance, the most serious and challenging responsibility she could have. And the maternal role is not only rewarding enough to stimulate and give her great satisfaction, but it also provides her with status and position in the community. Muslim women as a rule possess a deep certainty that this role has been entrusted to them because of their innate fitness and capacity for the most important of all tasks: the shaping of the future generation of humanity. Islam acknowledges the immensity of the debt which an individual owes to his parents, and especially to his mother, his first school in life, in many moving Quranic verses and *hadith* such as the following:

"And We have enjoined upon man concerning his parents: his mother carries him in weakness upon weakness, and his weaning is in two years. Therefore show gratitude to Me and to your parents: unto Me is the journeying." (31:14. also 46:15)

"Say: 'Come, I will recite to you what your Lord has made a sacred obligation for you: that you associate nothing with Him (as partner in his divinity) and that you do good to parents . . . .'"(6:151)

A man came to the Prophet (peace be on him) and said, "Messenger of God, I desire to go on a military expedition and I have come to consult you." He asked him if he had a mother and when he replied that he had, he said, "Stay with her, for Paradise is at her foot." (*hadith*)

Someone asked God's Messenger (peace be on him) to whom he should show kindness and he replied, "Your mother." He asked who came next and he replied, "Your mother." He asked who came next and he replied, "Your mother." He asked who came next and he replied, "Your father, then your relatives in order of relationship." (*hadith*)

The birth of a child is an event of great joy and thanksgiving which is shared by relatives and friends. It is *sunnah* to slaughter an animal when a baby is born and to feed friends and the poor with its meat as a token of thankfulness to God for the new family member. A male child must be circumcised at any time which is convenient without any attendant ceremonies.

Parents and their children are generally very close emotionally and physically. Breast feeding is considered the proper way to nourish a baby and nursing may be continued, if desired, for as long as two years. Mothers (and fathers as well) often sleep with their children when they are young in order to give them better care and more security, recognizing that the young child needs his mother as he needs food and air, not less during the night time than in the day. Leaving young children with baby-sitters or in nursery schools is a practice which, until quite recently was virtually unknown among Muslims. Children often accompany their parents, sharing in their experiences and pleasures and being part of their world, and if they must be left, as a rule they stay either with relatives, friends or trusted servants. Hence Muslim children generally grow up feeling very secure and loved, surrounded by a wide circle of family relationships within which they have a very secure place.

Training and guidance begin very early. Their goal is the molding of the child into a sound Islamic personality, with a good character and morals, strong Islamic principles, sound Islamic knowledge proper Islamic behavior, and the equipment to handle the demands of life in a responsible and mature fashion. Such training does not consist merely of a set of directives but, far more importantly, the parents' living example of unfailing submission to God through a sincere and conscientious practice of Islamic teachings. An essential part of this training, beginning very early in life, is obedience, respect and consideration for the parents themselves, as an embodiment of the well-known Muslim proverb, "The pleasure of God is the pleasure of the parents."

Islamic training aims, first, at giving the Muslim child a correct understanding of and relationship to Reality. He is taught very early that it does not consist merely of the material world which we observe and experience but of an unseen dimension as well, at the center of which is God Most High. God's absolute power and sovereignty, the human being's total dependence on Him and his place in the scheme of things, the existence of angels and also of satan and his forces, are all an essential part of this Reality. A child is able to understand all this, as well as the purpose of his life, the certainty of death and of returning to God when he or others die, and the future life in the garden or the fire, by the age of five or six, and it forms a vital part of his consciousness and comprehension of Reality as he grows up. At the same time, he is taught to love God, the Source of the innumerable blessings which fill his life, above everything, and that love and thankfulness to Him are best expressed in obedience to His commands. Meanwhile he learns about how God guides the human being through His messengers, and little by little the details of the guidance conveyed through Prophet Muhammad (peace be on him), whom he is taught to love above all other human beings, are imparted to him. Hence a sound conscience is developed early, and at a young age he is capable of being the watcher over his own actions.

As a result, when Muslim parents set guidelines for their child, he readily understands that the standards he is expected to follow are not just their own personal wishes but God's laws, to which the parents are subject just as much as he himself is. Conscientious Muslims naturally do their best to avoid behavior, activities and companions which do not fit in with a pure Islamic life and associate with sound practicing Muslims as much as possible. They see to it that their child has proper instruction in the teachings of Islam and encourage him to fulfill his Islamic obligations; they place him (insofar as they have any choice in the matter) in a school situation which is good for his total education and are careful about whom he associates with and what he is permitted to do, while at the same time encouraging wholesome activities and interests. Islamic training is total training: training in Islamic concepts, principles, attitudes, values, morals, manners and behavior. One reason why Muslims consider "family" so important, especially in selecting a spouse for their son or daughter, is because it is primarily the family which determines the sort of upbringing and breeding an individual will have; consequently a family of high standards and good repute can as a rule be depended upon to produce a young person—man or woman—of high quality.

As mentioned earlier, Muslim youngsters are considered by Islam as accountable to God for their own actions by the time they attain puberty. Therefore, at an age when in Western societies many young people are preoccupied with having a good time, personal appearance sex, drugs or drink, conscious Muslim young people are already highly responsible, fearing God in all they do and trying their best to stay away from what they know to be harmful and prohibited. By their middle 'teens, a boy is well-aware of his future role as the man of his household and is mentally preparing himself for it little by little, although he may not marry for several years, while a girl is readying herself for her future role as a wife, mother and homemaker, even though she may be continuing her studies for some time before she marries.

Today, when life in virtually every part of the world is confused by the pull of conflicting values and societal pressures, the conscientious Muslim youngster growing up in the Muslim world faces many challenges and problems. Many—perhaps most of the young people around him—are very far from Islam, often trying to lead him towards various things he knows are forbidden or not in keeping with his Islamic commitment; members of his own family may also be very far from Islam and may resent and attack his allegiance to it. And for a Muslim youngster growing up in America or other countries of the West, especially in the case of a girl, the situation is likely to be even more difficult. Throughout this time of great stress, the parents are the greatest source of support, understanding and guidance to Muslim young people, offering them a firm yet attainable example of what they are hoping and striving to become, and above all providing them with the love and warmth which constitute the strongest defense against the insecurity which prompts unhappy, unloved youngsters to search for solutions to their inner problems through illicit sex, alcohol, drugs or various deviant behaviors.

As the young adult Muslim man or woman gains experience and knowledge of life, works at a job, marries and has children of his or her own the love and devotion between children and parents is not in any way diminished. Now, through his own experiences, he realizes what they bore and sacrificed to bring him into the world and to raise him, especially if he has been brought up as a sound Muslim, and an adult-level sympathy and understanding now exists between them and him. And while there is a natural branching-off when a young man forms his own home with his wife or a girl goes to the home of her husband, the parents are not replaced in their affection by the newly formed relationship. For a Muslim son or daughter of any age, love for parents is not a once-a-year event to be announced with Mother's or Father's Day gifts or cards but a continuous and permanent state lasting as long as life itself endures. Although they may live in separate homes or localities, or even at the opposite ends of the earth, parents and children remain part of a single family unit whose members are bound together by the strongest ties of duty and affection.

As the parents get older and their vitality diminishes, this is not seen as the signal to put them away somewhere where they will not be a nuisance or make demands. In Muslim countries there is virtually no such institution as an old-age home; the aged are cared for by their children as a matter of course or by other relatives if there are no children. A Muslim does not regard this as a burden, no matter how demanding their care may be, but as an Islamic obligation, a duty he owes them. In the beautiful language of the Quran:

> *"Your Lord has commanded that you worship none but Him and that you be kind to parents. If either or both of them reach old age with you, do not say to them (so much as) 'Uff!' nor chide them but address them in terms of honor, and out of kindness lower to them your wing of humility and say, 'My lord, have mercy on them as they cherished me in childhood.'"*
> (17:23 94)

To the Muslim, the idea of putting old people into "homes" which are in reality custodial institutions where they go to vegetate and die in loneliness and despair so that one does not have to be burdened with their care seems totally barbarous and inhuman, a selfish ungrateful return for all they did for him when he was more helpless than they are now: he could never imagine that he would attain paradise if he did this to them — or to his parents-in-law or other aged relatives as well, who are just like parents for him. It is simply obvious and understood that when parents reach this stage of life, it is their children's turn to take care of them.

Thus the mutual love, compassion and sympathy between parents and children lasts throughout life, and when death comes to the parents, even though they were old and infirm and could long ago have been expected to die at any time, they are deeply and poignantly mourned and missed, and their example serves to inspire their children and grandchildren in time to come. Indeed, the duty of their children does not end with the death of the parents, for they continue to mention them in their prayers and to make supplication for God's mercy on them until the end of their own lives.

RELATIONS WITH RELATIVES

To a Muslim, close relations and kindness to other relatives is also very important. The grandparents are another mother and father who are to be treated just as one would treat his own parents, and aunts and uncles are regarded similarly. Sisters and brothers are usually very close, and their children are like one's own. Family ties are so close that it is not unusual for Muslims to assume responsibility for their younger brothers or sisters or for nieces and nephews or grandchildren if the need arises.[45]

If any of these relatives for instance, a grandparent, an elderly aunt or uncle, a widowed, divorced or unmarried sister, or an orphan are destitute, infirm or alone, these are as a rule provided for by some member of their family. In the Muslim world it is rare to find a person, man or woman, young or old, living by himself or herself, for people who are alone become the responsibility of one or another of their relatives, a member of their households, occupying a secure place in the family's life and in its regard rather than being left to struggle with the cares of life on their own.

Other forms of assistance to relatives when they need help are also very common. For example, if someone needs money, he does not go to a bank to get a loan at ten percent interest; instead he borrows it from one of his relatives, who does not refuse as long as he has it to lend, even though he may have other uses or needs for it himself, and of course, accepting interest is not only absolutely prohibited to Muslims but also absolutely unthinkable from a purely human perspective. "Binding ties of relationship" is considered very important in Islam, while hostility or breaking relations with relatives is a very serious matter. Hence, if there are conflicts or breaches among members of a family for any reason, the Muslim has a duty to act as a mediator and try to bring them together.

X.
RELATIONS BETWEEN THE SEXES

C ertain elements are basic to human nature, and one of these is the sexual urge. Every society has certain patterns of sexual behavior and these are never random. Invariably they reflect the society's value system and are a mirror of its basic attitudes toward human responsibility and accountability, the well-being of the family, and the purity and integrity of individuals and the society as a whole. The sexual mores of any society are therefore ultimately governed by its basic understanding of Reality, its fundamental attitudes concerning the origin and permanence of moral laws, and the human being's nature, role and responsibility in the world, as well as the nature and role of woman in society.

In a society which denies or which does not regulate its life by belief in God and obedience to His laws, the human being is regarded as a purely physical being who has a brief existence in this world. As there is nothing but the present life, it must be made the most of and enjoyed in every way possible before it ends, and no barriers or limits to enjoyment are acknowledged. Women and men are simply made to do what is "natural" without any significant moral or ethical considerations to hinder them.

In contrast, as we have seen, Islam emphatically rejects the notion that a human being is simply a physical or animal entity. Although it certainly does not deny that the human being has many needs and attributes which are common with animals, it does deny him the right to fulfill these needs in a purely animal fashion. Rather its aim is to regulate and channelize these animal aspects of human nature and to bring the whole of that nature, with its various facets and elements, into submission to God Most High.

As we saw earlier, the Islamic society is governed by a sense of both individual and collective responsibility to God Who has defined the limits for human behavior. Accordingly strong measures are taken to safeguard the purity and integrity of its individuals and institutions, especially the family. Again, Islam accords woman honor and dignity, and requires that she be treated with respect. Her sexuality may not be exploited in any way nor may she be treated as a sex object; rather she is to be regarded and treated as a human individual whose sexuality does not enter into her relationship with any person other than her husband. Not only does he have the exclusive right of sexual access to his wife but also the right that her beauty and feminine attractions should not be shared with other men, and the same is true of the wife in relation to her husband. Based on these general guidelines, Islam has established certain principles to govern the interaction of the sexes and control sexual behavior among Muslims.

The first of these principles is that free, casual social mixing between men and women is not permitted; in fact, mixing is discouraged unless it is for some serious, legitimate reason or purpose, not simply as a means of amusing oneself or enjoying the company of the opposite sex. For this reason, in many parts of the Muslim world, schools, colleges, hospitals, transportation facilities, etc., have separate sections for men and women. Homes are often constructed in such a way that men who visit the house do not come in contact with its women; male visitors are received by the men of the house and entertained in a guest room, while the women carry on their own activities in their informal home attire in other parts of the house without being seen by the visitors or inconvenienced in any way. Likewise, women also have their circle of female friends, and when these come to visit, they in turn do not mix with the men of the household.

The second principle is that when mixing does take place, both men and women are to exercise propriety in the way they speak, look and behave. Obviously a woman can be either business-like and direct, or she can let her sexuality into the picture in her interaction with men in innumerable implicit and overt ways. This Muslim women are not permitted to do. At the same time, men are expected to exercise the same restraint in behavior, not to look deliberately and with interest at women's attractions, to be playful or "friendly" with them, or to have any physical contact with them whatsoever, but to keep the interaction strictly straight-forward and direct.

The third principle regulating the relations between the sexes in Islam is that a Muslim man and woman who are not related either by marriage or by a *mahram* relationship are not permitted to be alone together. A well-known *hadith* of the Prophet (peace be on him) states, "Whoever believes in God and the last day should not sit in privacy with a woman without a *mahram* of hers being present, because satan will be the third (among them to lead them into temptation)."

How vividly this describes just what occurs when a man and woman are alone together, when the consciousness of their sexuality creeps in between them, affecting their relationship and making them feel for one another what should not be felt, disturbing their inner equilibrium and purity and leading them toward the possibility of sin. Thus, even when a Muslim man or woman meets with a prospective marriage partner, although they may see and talk with one another in the presence of *mahram* relatives, Islam forbids their going out or staying alone with each other on the principle that if there is no occasion for temptation there will likewise be no occasion for wrongdoing.

The fourth principle is that the Muslim woman is required to conceal her attractions from men by a strictly modest, straight-forward type of attire. Within the close family circle, she is free to dress informally and to beautify herself; in fact, she is strongly encouraged to make herself attractive for her husband since her beauty is reserved for him. She is also free to do the same among other Muslim women if no man is present. But outside her home and at any time when she is in the presence of non-*mahram* men, even within her home, she is required to wear a covering-type of dress which will make it clear to anyone who sees her that she is a chaste, modest and pure woman, and that she does not want her sexuality to enter into the interaction in the slightest degree.

A Muslim woman in this business-like non-attracting kind of dress which brings out her femininity while concealing her sexuality and with correspondingly straight-forward behavior, automatically elicits and receives the respect of men just as nuns, whose habits are somewhat similar to the covering dress of Muslim women, have always been respected. This type of dress, which is known as *hijab* or *purdah*, is prescribed by a direct order in the Quran and is a characteristic by which a conscientious Muslim woman is recognizable anywhere in the world. We will have more to say on this subject in the section on clothing.

It is within this context that the Islamic concept of womanhood may be understood most clearly. The respect and status which a Muslim woman enjoys are not tied up in any way with her physical attractiveness or social skills in relation to men: rather it is concealing and reserving her beauty and sexuality, her feminine charms and favors, exclusively for the man she has married which marks her as a virtuous woman and gains her respect. Indeed, Islam prescribes *hijab* not only to protect society from the disruption produced by uncontrolled expressions of sexual interest and in order to protect woman's dignity and honor, but also in order to neutralize her sexuality so that she can be a positive, constructive force in society rather than a harmful one.

Due to this modest dress and the propriety of her manner and behavior, men can regard and treat her as a person, not a sex object: that is, her value to the society has no relationship to her physical attractions but solely to her worth as a human being. Consequently, as a Muslim woman grows older she loses none of her value either in her own eyes or in the sight of society, for a Muslim woman's worth, like a man's, increases with age due to her wisdom and experience instead of decreasing with her declining youthfulness and beauty. For the Muslim woman, her character and personal attainments, her modesty and dignity, her piety and intelligence, and her feminine role as wife and mother are the sources of status and respect within the community rather than her possessing sexual interest, attractiveness or easy sociability with men.

But lest it be thought that the responsibility for maintaining pure relations with the opposite sex rests with women alone, we have only to cite the following well-known Quranic verse:

> *"Tell the believing men to lower their gaze[46] and guard their sexuality; that is purer for them Indeed. God is aware of what they do. And tell the believing women to lower their gaze and guard their sexuality . . . ."* (24:30-31)

The Islamic teachings thus inculcate in men and women alike a strong sense of *haya*, that is, shyness, reserve and modesty in the presence of the opposite sex (and indeed, in relation to modesty, of one's own sex as well), which acts as a very strong deterrent against indecency. Due to this, a conscious Muslim man avoids just as scrupulously as his Muslim sister anything which would lead him toward what is forbidden or would lower him in his own eyes or before his Lord: likewise his dress and manner demonstrate that he possesses self-respect and is free of indecent intentions and desires.[47] In short, chastity, modesty and purity are not merely external restraints imposed by religion or society but are rather inner qualities which devout Muslim men as well as women deeply cherish and desire to uphold.

It will be obvious from this that Muslims generally do not feel at ease with the current trends in Western society .Conscientious Muslims who come to visit or to live in Western countries are often deeply shocked by the general lack of shame and modesty by the fact that illicit sex is no longer censured in the society as a whole. They regard the open display of flesh and the overt sexual behavior which they see all around them as animalistic and degrading. The fact that sexual undertones can be observed in innumerable aspects of the interaction between men and women in Western society—between a professor and his student, a doctor and his patient, or a boss and a secretary in an office, for example, and between neighbors, friends and even relatives—in the form of the off-color joke, the compliments, the back-patting, the constant undercurrent of sexually tinged innuendo which one encounters on so many occasions is also very distressing to them.

Among Muslims, apart from the very westernized and others, primarily young people, who have lost their sense of direction, such behavior is very rare indeed; certainly the interaction of men and women who fear God and strictly observe His limits is completely free of these elements. The observing of the limits informs both the man and the woman that there is no place and no wish for anything to do with sex in their interaction; indeed, if there were such undertones it would be felt as a great threat as well as a gross insult, and would render further interaction prohibited and impossible. To a conscious Muslim man or woman, attention from any member of the opposite sex other than one's own spouse in the form of free talk, compliments, playfulness, suggestive comments, touching in any form (including handshaking and patting on the back), and anything else which has sexual undertones is insulting, degrading and very much disliked.

In summary, Islam regards the sexual urge as an extremely powerful element in human nature, one which clamors for free expression if given even slight encouragement. Without such guidelines and limits for governing it as we have just discussed, and without the certainty that such behavior is forbidden and will be very severely punished in the hereafter, it will naturally seek to express itself freely, as we see in Western societies. Recognizing the strength of this drive and the fact that it is always present in any situation where men and women interact freely with one another, are alone together, and where bodies are exposed, Islam does not permit any of these things; for it is obviously far more desirable and effective as well as much more realistic to prevent temptation than to expect people to resist it when circumstances impel them toward it. Islam also insists on the right of an individual to have a spouse who belongs exclusively to him/her; that is, one whose body has not been tasted and enjoyed by the eyes or the hands of others. It totally rejects the notion that what people feel for each other or the pleasure they derive from an act should be taken as the criteria of right and wrong, and that obedience to the unbridled demands of animal desires should be permitted to dominate the lives of human beings. The moral and spiritual harm done to individuals, and through them to their society, when they disregard the vital need of the human personality for purity and integrity to follow blind physical desire, cannot be assessed by anyone but God, Who has so clearly and absolutely prohibited such acts, and Who has also informed us the awesome penalties which such proscribed deeds will incur in the life-to-come.

XI.

DAILY LIFE

As we pointed out earlier, in Islam the broad meaning of worship is not confined to so-called religious observances such as praying and fasting. Rather everything which people do in keeping with Gods laws in order to satisfy their legitimate needs and those of their families or society is considered worship, broadening its definition to include all one does with the intention of pleasing God in any aspect of life. Without this overall intention of pleasing and obeying God no deeds no matter how "good" they may be in content or results are acceptable to or will be rewarded by God, for they have been done for some motive other than obtaining His pleasure and hence the reward of them has been sought and often found elsewhere.

For the conscious Muslim the Holy Quran and the *sunnah* of the Prophet (peace be on him) are the guide in all aspects of existence. The Quran is a book of life which he opens several times daily either the printed Book itself or that portion of it which he has committed to memory turning to it again and again both during *salah* and at other times as well for guidance, understanding support, comfort and the remembrance of God Most High. Similarly the Prophet's *sunnah* (his words and deeds) is a vital, living example which he tries his best to follow in all matters,

177

small and great, knowing that no other pattern of conduct or life could be as worthy to be emulated as that of the noble, inspired Messenger of God (may His peace and blessings be on him).

With this in mind, we now turn our attention to the application of Islam to basic aspects of human life.

WORK AND STRIVING

Work and striving in the worldly realm are a very important part of the Muslim's practice of Islam. Since administering the affairs of the earth in the best possible manner is the human being's responsibility, managing its resources, developing science, industry, technology, human potential and abilities, and mastering the entire multitude of skills necessary for the effective and smooth running of society are a religious obligation. All this can only come about by the expenditure of sincere and dedicated effort. The Quran is explicit in stating that God's help comes only to those who work and strive with commitment and sincerity:

> *"And those who strive hard for Us,We will most certainly guide them in Our paths. for Verily God is with those who do right."* (29:69)

> *" And we shall try you until We have known those among you who strive hard and who are patient, and until We test your record."* (47:31)

> *". . . . that the human being has nothing but what he strives for, and that his striving will be seen, and that afterwards he will be repaid for it with the fullest repayment, and that to the Lord is the goal."* (53:39-42)

Hence Islam respects honest effort and work of any kind and does not consider any necessary or useful endeavor as degrading. If a need for some service or skill is felt by the Muslim community, whether it be for a high-level scientist or someone to collect the garbage, it becomes an obligation on some members of the society to master whatever knowledge or skills may be necessary and to engage in this work. And whatever is done should be done in the best and most excellent manner possible, in keeping with the Prophet's saving, "God loves that when any of you does anything, he should do it in the best way." The only prohibited endeavors are those which are connected with prohibited activities, i.e., making a living by gambling, earning interest, magic or fortune-telling, pornography, prostitution or any other form of sexual contact or display, and by anything related to the production or consumption of alcohol, harmful drugs or pork. And while Islam does not prohibit women from working, they are not permitted to do so in situations where they come in casual contact with men, are exposed to temptations or degradation of any sort, or where their bodies become the focus of interest or their modesty is affected.

In the Islamic system of life, every member of the community must contribute whatever he or she is capable of for the good of society, whether it is a child or youth who is studying in order to master necessary knowledge or skills, a woman in her role as the manager of her household, or a man with whatever abilities,physical or intellectual, he may possess. Islam is not a system which permits praying or meditating all day long or living the life of an ascetic while making no effort either for oneself or for others. Once the Prophet (peace be on him) was told about a man who spent all his time in the mosque praying. He asked, "Then who feeds him?"

"His brother," was the reply.

"Then his brother is better than he," he said, underscoring the point that the religion of Islam does not consist merely of piety and devotional activities but also of hard work and reliance upon one's own efforts. Even the most pious and devout of the Prophet's Companions, with the exception of a handful of men who devoted themselves exclusively to worship and the study of Islam, had an occupation or calling of some sort. Many of them were engaged in trade or business, as was the Prophet himself earlier in life. For example, Abu Bakr Siddiq and Uthman bin Affan, two of the Prophet's closest friends who became the first and third caliphs of Islam after his death, acquired considerable wealth through the prospering of their businesses, despite which they lived with the most extreme simplicity and austerity, and from time to time gave away virtually everything they possessed for the cause of Islam.

Thus, while Islam has made it the responsibility of Muslims to take care of people who for any reason are unable to meet their own needs through *zakah* and voluntary charity it certainly does not encourage living off handouts from any source. Again, although Muslims are not supposed to turn away anyone who asks. begging. especially by one who is able to work., is considered degrading and harmful. The Prophet (peace be on him) said. "It is better for one of you to take his rope, bring a load of firewood on his back and sell it. God thereby preserving his self respect than that he should beg from people whether they give him anything or refuse him. This underlines the respectability of any type of useful work and the undesirability of living by the labor of others or by charity whether it comes from individuals, organizations or the government. Islam is thus a realistic system for living which condemns idleness, prohibits asceticism and discourages begging, for it makes it clear that a human being's dignity and sense of self-worth, as well as the well-being of society, are intimately tied up with sincere and honest effort, not merely of some but all of its members.

KNOWLEDGE

Islam's attitude toward the pursuit of knowledge and education is summarized in the following Quranic verses and *hadith* of the Prophet (peace be on him):

> ". . . . *And say (O Muhammad): 'My Lord, increase me in knowledge.'*" (20:114)

> "*Is one who worships devoutly during the hours of the night prostrating himself or standing, who takes heed of the hereafter and who places his hope in the mercy of his Lord (like one who does not)? Say: 'Are they equal, those who know*

and those who do not?' It is those who are embued with under-
standing who receive admonition." (39:9)

"Seeking knowledge is a duty on every Muslim man and
woman."(*hadith*)

"Seek knowledge even if you have to go to China."
(*hadith*)

The Prophet (peace be on him) prayed, "O my Lord, do
not let the sun set on any day during which I did not increase
in knowledge." (*hadith*)

"No gift among all the gifts of a father to his child is better than education." (*hadith*)

The most essential knowledge which a Muslim should seek
before everything else, is a correct understanding of Reality and
the precepts of Islam, for upon this knowledge all his life and
deeds depend. However, secular knowledge is also of great
importance and should not be neglected. These two branches of
knowledge, of spiritual matters and of the world's life, should be
studied and mastered side by side, each supplementing and com-
plementing the other, as was done in earlier times in the Muslim
world, so that there may be no schism or conflict between
"sacred" and "secular" matters, between the realm of the world
and spirit, either within the Muslim's personality and behavior or
within his society.

Knowledge is to be sought both for its own sake, for the love
of learning and for its applications. It is the duty of those who
have knowledge to impart it to others. According to a *hadith*, a
Muslim who has gone out or is traveling in search of knowledge
is "in the way of God until he returns."

There are, however, various types of knowledge inspired by
satan which Muslims are not permitted to learn or to engage in,
such as magic and the black arts, fortune-telling, astrology, and
anything related to immorality or wickedness. And while

Muslims are assuredly permitted to acquire the knowledge of science, technology and the like from non-Muslim sources, they are not permitted to acquire together with this knowledge the values and behavior of people or societies which are not ruled by a strict sense of accountability to God. Rather they are to subject whatever practical and scientific knowledge they acquire to the Islamic criteria and standards, to apply whatever is appropriate and beneficial toward the building of an Islamic society governed by God's laws in all aspects of life, and to leave alone whatever is not appropriate or useful.

MONEY AND POSSESSIONS

Islam freely acknowledges the existence of the human being's attraction to the material sphere—his love of wealth and possessions, houses and lands, buying and selling and acquiring things. It does not prohibit any of these, but it does require that he keep a correct perspective concerning their relative importance so that the things of this life do not become the object of his existence or his goal. The Quran says:

> *"Alluring to people is the love of things they covet women sons, hoarded treasures of gold and silver, highly-bred horses, cattle and land. This is the provision of this world's life. Yet with God is a better abode."* (3:14)

> *"And whatever things you have been given are but the provision of this world's life and its adornment. and that which is with God is better and more enduring. Have you then no understanding."* (28:60)

Accordingly, the Muslim is permitted to acquire wealth and property and to enjoy the use of his possessions: however, this is to be balanced with a sense of proportion and moderation. He must not become so involved with these things or with any sorts of worldly concerns that they interfere with his relationship with God or cause him to lose sight of the purpose of his existence and his ultimate destination. Moreover, the rights of God and of the less fortunate on his wealth in the form of the obligatory *zakah* and voluntary charity are not to be forgotten. For all of an individual's wealth and possessions are a gift and a trust from God, not his by right or simply due to his own efforts or merits but to God's beneficence. As such, they are to he spent not only for oneself and one's family but also to help others who are in want or distress as well. And whatever a Muslim spends from his means for those in need or in the way of God is a *"goodly loan"* to God which He will repay with great increase in the hereafter. In passage after passage the Quran speaks about giving and spending for others:

". . . .Those who go in awe for fear of their lord, and those who believe in their Lord s revelations, and those who do not ascribe partners to their Lord, and those who give that which they give with hearts afraid because they are about to return to their Lord these race (with one another) for the good things, and they shall win them in the race." (23:57-61)

"You will not attain righteousness until you spend out of that which you love. And whatever you spend from (your) possessions, indeed God is aware of it." (3:92)

"Those who spend their wealth by night and by day in secret and in the open their reward is from their Lord, and no fear shall be on them nor shall they grieve." (2:274)

These Islamic teachings inculcate in Muslims a basic attitude of generosity and open-handedness due to which, as a rule, they spend freely for others and money never becomes an issue or object of discussion among them: it is simple to be used, for others as much as for oneself. After all, which of us can be said to own anything? Today I spend for you, and tomorrow or on some other occasion when the need arises or it is appropriate, you spend for me.

At the same time, Islam discourages wastefulness indulgence in unreasonable luxuries, and spending for show or to impress others. Simplicity, contentment and thankfulness for whatever God has seen fit to bestow on one are important qualities, while pride in one's wealth, a sense of being above others who have less, greed or miserliness are very great sins. Money is of value only for what it can do, not for itself. It is therefore not to be hoarded or allowed to sit idle in the form of savings but is either to be spent for legitimate needs or to help others, or to be kept in circulation by appropriate and beneficial investment.

FOOD AND EATING

Like the other good things of life, food and drink are not to be taken for granted. Rather they are to be accepted with thankfulness as the bounty of God and to be used wisely and for the maintenance of health. The Prophet (peace be on hint) said that the Muslims are those who do not eat unless they are hungry and when they eat they do not fill themselves. Again, he said that one third of the stomach is for food, one-third for liquids, and one third for air, all pointing to moderation in food habits and to the desirability of eating to maintain physical well-being rather than simply for enjoyment, although food is certainly meant to be enjoyed as well.

The Muslim pronounces the name of God (*bismillah ar-rahman ar-raheem*, in the Name of God, the Merciful, the Compassionate) when he begins to eat or drink, just as when he begins any other undertaking, and ends his meal with brief words of thanksgiving to God. Muslims consider it a blessing to have guests to share their food, and they are renowned for their hospitality which is at the same time an Islamic obligation This comes from the deep conviction that it is God Who feeds all creatures, not this or that person: all will eat, both host and guest, whether by one person's means or another's. One person's food is sufficient for two, the Prophet (peace be on him) said, the food of two is sufficient for four and the food of four sufficient for eight; for where there is true brotherliness and goodwill, food can be stretched indefinitely so that all who are hungry can have a share. In the same way one's house and the food in it do not belong exclusively to the host, but also to the guest who shares it.

Among Muslims it is customary to tell a visitor to their home, in effect, "Brother or sister, this house is your house, so please feel at home." It is customary that this is for three days.

Islam regards wasting food as a sin and an indication of contempt for Gods precious gifts and bounties, which makes even such a seemingly small thing as throwing away a piece of bread or treading on crumbs an impious act. Consequently, in Muslim countries if leftover food is not stored, it is as a rule given to servants, to needy people or beggars, or to animals who also require food, in keeping with the Prophet's example, rather than being thrown away.

Which foods and drinks are permitted to Muslims and which are prohibited? As we saw earlier, in Islam the principle is that whatever is not specifically (or by analogy) prohibited is permissible; hence all foods and drinks are allowed except the following which are prohibited in the Quran: (1) anything which intoxicates or interferes with the clear functioning of the mind, in any quantity or form; (2) pork and its by-products in any form; (3) the flesh of animals which have died without being slaughtered and bled fully (with the exception of game animals), those which have been killed by a blow, by falling from a height or by being gored with horns; (4) blood; and (5) any food over which the name of deity other than God has been invoked and the meat of an animal slaughtered in the name of anyone other than God. To this list may be added, by analogy, birds of prey, animals with claws and fangs, rodents and reptiles, and insects with the exception of locusts. All seafood is permissible according to the majority of schools of law; nothing is specified about the manner of killing them and the restrictions applying to meat do not apply to them.

The manner of slaughtering an animal prescribed by Islam is to slit its throat in a swift and merciful manner, saying "*Bismillah*, Allahu *Akbar*" (In the Name of God, God is greater) in acknowledgment that the life of this creature of God is taken by His permission to meet one's lawful need for food; the animal is then bled completely. Consequently many Muslims living in non-Muslim countries where God's name is not pronounced at the time of slaughter or where animals are slaughtered in a different manner consider commercial meat to be unlawful to Muslims, and they either have access to a Muslim or a kosher meat service, slaughter their own animals from time to time, or do without meat.

Another opinion holds that since the Quran is quite explicit in stating that the food of Christians and Jews is lawful for Muslims, Muslims who live in Christian countries may eat commercial meat (apart from pork), pronouncing God's name on it at the time of eating. Today Muslim butchers and meat services are becoming increasingly common in Western countries in order that Muslims may have meat slaughtered according to Islamic prescription.

For those who invite Muslims to eat in their homes, it may be useful to list here the principal food which conscientious Muslims avoid. These include alcohol, both as a beverage and in foods[48] and pork and its by-products; these are, apart from meat, primarily its fat[49] and gelatin.[50] Conscientious Muslims living in the West, and even in Muslim countries into which packaged foods are imported from outside, must read the ingredients of all packages to avoid these substances, and they often experience problems eating in restaurants, airplanes, hospitals, schools, etc.

People often wonder why pork has been prohibited. It should be noted that it was prohibited to the Jews in the Law revealed to Moses, and Jesus and his disciples, as devout followers of this scripture, also strictly adhered to this prohibition. It was not until after Paul proclaimed the Mosaic Law to be abolished that Christians began to regard this and other provisions of that Law to have been set aside. As prohibition by Islam, the reason for it is not mentioned either in the Quran or the *Hadith*. However, the prohibition is very explicit:

> *"Forbidden to you (as food) are carrion and blood and swineflesh, and that which has been dedicated to any other than God and the strangled, and the dead through beating, and the dead through falling from a height, and that which has been killed by (the goring of) horns, and that which has been*

*devoured by wild beasts except that which you make lawful (by
killing it while it is still alive), and that which has been immo-
lated to idols . . . "* (5:4, also 2:173, 6:145, 16:115)

This makes is very clear that in the knowledge of the Creator
there is something exceedingly filthy and harmful in the flesh of
swine which renders it totally unfit for human consumption placing it among other things which no one would consider as clean
food. In 6:145 the prohibition is reiterated, characterizing swine-
flesh as something *"that verily is foul...."* This is quite understandable in view of the fact that pigs are the dirtiest of animals
and that they feed upon every type of filth which in turn becomes
part of every cell of their bodies, they are also the carriers of a
dangerous disease, trichinosis. In any case, whether the reason
for the prohibition is known or not known, Muslims try to obey
it faithfully, realizing that not all animals—even domesticated
ones—are suitable for food even though the flesh may be good-
tasting and readily available, and that the All Wise, All-Knowing
Creator is infinitely better aware of what is for the good of His
creation than the human being with his extremely limited perception and knowledge ever can be.

DRESS

Islam places great stress on cleanliness, hygiene and respect
for the bodies God gave to human beings, for God *"shaped
you and made your shapes beautiful"* (40:64, 64:3). As we
have seen, cleanliness and ritual purification of the body is a prerequisite for the performance of *salah* and in addition to this
Islam insists on a very high standard of personal hygiene. There
are many *hadith* in which the Prophet (peace be on him) enjoined
on Muslims to be clean, neat, respectful of their bodies by taking
care of them properly, and attentive to appearance, while dis-
couraging unkemptness in dress and grooming, especially among
those who are able to afford good clothes, for "God likes to see
the signs of His bounty on His servants." (*hadith*)

It is a natural human desire to want to adorn oneself and

one's surroundings with what is beautiful, one which Islam acknowledges and permits, with certain limitations. Accordingly, Muslims are permitted to beautify themselves with nice clothing, jewelry, perfume and the like, but for women these are to be worn only in the presence of their husbands, immediate family members or other Muslim women without, however, becoming very engrossed in or spending excessive amounts of time on these matters. What a Muslim woman wears among women or in her home when no non-*mahram* men are present depends upon her taste and inclination in keeping with basic Islamic standards of modesty For her husband alone she may make herself attractive in any way she likes.

We now return to the subject of *hijab*, the covering dress of Muslim women Many people wonder why religion should have anything to say about dress as this appears to them to belong to the realm of personal taste. But as we have seen Islam is not a system which concerns itself merely with the human individual's soul or inner dimension while ignoring his body, the external aspect. Rather it regards the human being as an indivisible whole and addresses itself to the totality of his life, requiring that the Muslim be a Muslim, reflecting the Islamic teachings, God's laws for mankind, with his entire being. This obviously includes appearance and dress the keynote of which, as we have seen, is to be strict modesty in public.

Hence *hijab* is not an isolated aspect of the Muslim women's life but fits in with and reinforces the Islamic social system, and in particular the Islamic concept of womanhood Just as Western forms of' dress have developed from and fit the world-view societal values and conception of womanhood of Western civilization so does the dress of Muslim women emanate from and fit the Islamic value system and view of life. Yet *hijab* is not merely a kind of covering dress but more importantly, something which the Muslim woman keeps about her soul and consciousness at all times to act as a barrier or curtain of *haya* between herself and the men with whom she comes in contact.. As such, it is in fact the totality of her property and modesty in behavior, manner, speech and appearance.

Then just what is the Islamic dress of women supposed to look like? The Quran enjoins:

> *"And tell the believing women to lower their gaze and guard their sexuality, and to display of their adornment only what is apparent*[51] *and to draw their head coverings over their bosoms."* (24:30)

And,

> *"O Prophet, tell your wives and daughters and the believing woman to draw their outer garments around them (when they go out or are among men). That is better, in order that they may be understood (to be muslims) and not annoyed . . . ."* (33:59)

The characteristics of the Islamic dress are therefore laid down by the above verses and by a *hadith* of the Prophet (peace be on him) which states, "Whenever a woman begins to menstruate, it is not right that anything should be seen except this and this and this," and the Prophet pointed to his face and hands. Consequently, while Islam does not specify a particular style of form of dress, what is required is that a woman should be completely covered except for her hands and face and that her dress should conceal her form, be loose and non-transparent and not of a kind to attract attention by its beauty; moreover cosmetics perfume and jewelry (with the exception of what ordinarily shows such as a ring) are not to be worn in public. The dress of Muslim woman should not be an imitation of the dress of men, and it should be such that the wearer can be clearly recognized as a Muslim.

Looking around the Muslim world we find an amazing variety of garments which meet these requirements. The clothes of woman differ from country to country and in some countries even differ from region to region or among various groups within the same country Muslim women are in no was constrained to wear a particular form of dress and are free to improve on or

invent new types of dresses in keeping with the Islamic guidelines as dictated by convenience or taste. However, whatever is
worn should be a full and honest Islamic *hijab* which clearly
reflects the wearer's Islamic identity, not an apologetic one or
one which meets only part of the requirements. The Holy Prophet
(peace be on him) very strongly condemned women who appear
naked while then are fully clothed."

This is the Islamic ideal. However, Western dress is now so
common in many parts of the Muslim world that many Muslim
woman (and men as well) have never worn anything except
Western clothes even in their own countries. Most are aware, to
a greater or lesser extent, that Islam requires the wearing of *hijab*
but then do not wear it for a variety of reasons, primarily because
they are afraid of being considered "different" or "backward" if
they do.

Others wear *hijab* but since then lack an adequate understanding of Islam as a total system of life, they regard it as more
of a societal tradition than an Islamic obligation; when they make
a trip outside or go to live in a Western country, they often
remove their covering, not wanting to attract attention or appear
different from others. Still other woman—a large and rapidly
increasing number—wear *hijab* and maintain it wherever they
may happen to go, convinced that what is required is modesty,
whether it is "different" or not, and concerned with gaining the
pleasure and approval of their Lord rather than of the people,
with pride and confidence in their Islamic identity and attire.
Consequently today in America and other countries of the West
one can see many Muslim women, indigenous as well as foreign,
clad in various forms of *hijab* as an integral expression of their
faith.

People often suppose that it must be very difficult or impossible to move about freely or do work clad in such a dress.[52] This
is not the case, as the vast numbers of Muslim women of all levels and walks of life who wear such clothing in virtually every
country of the world can testify. Today numerous high school and
university students, teachers, doctors and other women who hold
important and responsible jobs in all areas are voluntarily adopt-

ing Islamic dress as being a vital expression of their Islamic identity. They lead very active and busy lives, *hijab* constituting no
impediment to their work or freedom of movement. They do not
regard wearing it as a hardship; on the contrary, they feel safe and
protected because of it and would not exchange it for any other
form of dress. For this modest attire protects the Muslim woman
from the sexual interest and improper looks and behavior of men;
wearing it, she can move about in the world as necessity requires
with dignity and a complete consciousness of her own propriety
and modesty (it is obviously a bit difficult to feel really modest
in clothing which was designed for anything except the purpose
of modesty, no matter how modest one's intentions may be!) as
well as of her clear Islamic identity, in obedience to her Lord's
commands.[53]

Then what about the dress of Muslim men? Does Islam have
nothing to say concerning it? Yes, it does. First of all, modesty
requires that the area between the navel and the knee not be
exposed in front of anyone, including other males, excepting
one's wife. The clothing of men should not be tight or sexually
provocative, nor should it resemble the dress of women. In addition, it is not supposed to be an imitation of the dress of others so
that Muslims may at all times retain their distinctive Islamic
identity and character. The wearing of gold and silk, which are
reserved for women is not permitted to Muslim men. Although in
many parts of the Muslim world Western dress is common
among men, nevertheless there are many different and distinctive
types of male as well as female dress. And while most Muslim
men living in the West wear Western dress in public in their
homes and for various occasions they often wear their traditional dress which has also been adopted by many Western converts
to Islam.

XII.
HUMAN RELATIONSHIPS

The Muslim acknowledging one Creator sees humanity as one all equally His creatures for the Quran says:

> *"And among His signs is the creation of the heavens and the earth and the variations in your languages and your colors. Indeed in that are signs for those who know."* (30:22)

> *"O mankind We created you from a single male and female and made you into nations and tribes that you may know each other. Verily, the most honored of you before God is the most righteous of you And God is Knower Aware."* (49:13)

Thus to the Muslim, the colors, races and languages of human beings the obvious external differences within the human family are signs of God's wondrous creativity, the God-ordained diversity of mankind within its overall unity. Such outward differences can never constitute a reason for either looking up to or despising another individual, for the only criteria Islam acknowledges for distinction or greatness among human beings are spiritual and moral qualities such as the degree of faith and God-consciousness, the excellence of a person's character, and his level of knowledge and practice of Islam. Worldly considerations such as wealth, status, power, family and education do not count at all in the sight of God unless an individual uses them to follow His guidance and seek His pleasure.

Within the human family, those who hold the same view of Reality and possess the same values will naturally feel the greatest closeness and affinity to one another. Consequently the Muslim, whether living in the Muslim world or anywhere else, will naturally find his greatest source of support, affection and kindred feeling among other Muslims. Regardless of their national origin, language or cultural habits, the followers of Islam form one community. Like the members of a single family, they care for one another's needs and share good and bad times; they provide each other with encouragement in living Islam and act as a deterrent in deviating from it. The tone for the mutual relationship among Muslims is set by many Quranic verses and *Hadith*:

> *"And the believers, men and women, are protecting friends to one another. They enjoin what is right and forbid what is wrong, they observe regular salah and pay zakah, and they obey God and His Messenger. As for these God will hare mercy on them. Verily God is Mighty, Wise."* (9:71)

> *"It is He Who strengthened you (the Prophet) with His help and with the believers, and He has put affection between their hearts. If you had spent all that is in the earth, you could not have produced that affection in their hearts, but God has produced that affection between them."* (8:69-63)

> "The believers are brothers Then make peace between your brothers and remain conscious of God that you may obtain mercy." (49 10)

> "The believers are like a single person: if his eye is affected all of him is affected, and if his head is affected all of him is affected." (*hadith*)

> "The believers are to one another like a building whose

parts support one another."(*hadith*)

> "None of you has believed until he loves for his brother what he loves for himself." (*hadith*)

Beyond this circle of his brothers and sisters-in-faith, to the Muslim all human beings are brothers- and sisters-in-humanity, and the same obligation of kindness, fairness and consideration are due to them all. Islam does not permit discrimination in the treatment of other human beings on the basis of religion or any other criteria. Indeed, Islam's insistence on fairness and good treatment to all human beings without differentiation is so strong that it prohibits Muslims from behaving with cruelty or malice even toward the people of the enemy in time of war. In particular, it emphasizes neighborliness and respect for the ties of relationship with non-Muslims, following the example and injunctions of the Prophet (peace be on him). The tone for the Muslim's relations with other human beings regardless of their faith is set in the following *hadith*, among many others:

> "All creatures are God's children, and those dearest to God are the ones who treat His children kindly." (*hadith*)

> "The believer is not the one who eats his fill when his neighbor beside him is hungry." (*hadith*)

> "He from whose injurious conduct his neighbor is not safe will not enter paradise." (*hadith*)

Within this human family, Jews and Christians, who share many beliefs and values with Muslims, constitute what Islam terms *ahl al-kitab*, that is, People of the Scripture, and hence Muslims have a special kind of relationship to them. Islam permits Muslims to eat the food of Christians and Jews (except of course what is expressly forbidden, notably pork, which conscientious Jews avoid just as scrupulously as Muslims, and alcohol) and Muslim men are allowed to marry women of these faiths. We will now take a closer look at some vital aspects of the relationship between Muslims, Jews and Christians in human terms and at the similarities and differences of Islam with their respective faiths.

RELATIONS WITH JEWS

*A*hl al-kitab denotes those people to whom God conveyed His guidance through a divine Scripture or Book revealed to His prophets. In the case of Jews, this scripture is the Torah or Pentateuch, the revelation bestowed on Prophet Moses (God's peace and blessings be on him). However, this is not to be understood as the Torah (the first five books of the Old Testament) in its present form. Even a casual examination of these books makes it clear that, although they may originally have been based on a divine message, they were actually authored by human beings, since they contain innumerable marked inconsistencies, discrepancies and factual errors, as well as much subject matter which does not fit the criteria for a divinely revealed scripture.[54] Moreover, these books constitute primarily a religious, political and social history of the Children of Israel rather than a scripture conveying such clear spiritual and moral guidance, as well as accurate information concerning the true nature of Reality, as could have come only from the Lord of all creation.

Many elements, particularly the uncompromising stress on the Oneness of God and His guidance through the prophets, are common between Judaism and Islam, as one would naturally expect since both come from the same divine Source. All the early prophets of the Old Testament are mentioned by name in the Quran and they are held in the greatest respect by Muslims. There are also many similarities in values, morals and living habits between the two faiths and Jews lived for centuries under Islamic rule enjoying full religious rights.

However, the problem of Israel has greatly damaged relations between Muslims and Jews, although the issue does not involve religious questions *per se*. It is natural and obvious that Muslims strongly deplore and oppose Zionist expansion in the name of Judaism, into Muslim and Arab areas, for Israel has laid claim to territories where Muslims have lived for centuries, some parts of which are as sacred to the followers of Islam as they are to the followers of Judaism and Christianity, holding them to be an integral part of the Jewish homeland, as well as essential to Israel's security. Regarding the notion of a Jewish homeland, we read in the Jewish Torah that God said to Abraham (peace be on him):

> *"And I will give to you and to your posterity after you the land in which you are a stranger, all the land of Canaan (Palestine) for an everlasting possession, and I will be their God."* (Genesis 17:8)

That the descendants of Abraham include Muslims as well as Jews is incontestable; therefore if the issue had really been related to and determined by God's promise referred to in this passage from the scripture of the Jews themselves, there would be no problem. As is well-known, Jews and Muslims had been living peacefully side by side for centuries in the land which God promised to the posterity of Abraham until the Muslims were dispossessed in recent times by the establishment of Israel. Hence this claim is simply a cover for naked aggression and the unconcealed desire for territorial expansion and conquest.

As we have seen, Islam does not permit Muslims to compromise with injustice and oppression. Since fighting for the basic human right to one's life, freedom, home and property is an Islamic obligation, they cannot remain passive while their people are killed or expelled from their homes and their lands are confiscated for no other cause than that they are wanted by someone else. The issue is therefore not in any sense one of religious disagreement—for none whatever exists in that respect but rather a moral issue in which truth, justice and freedom from oppression are at stake.

RELATIONS WITH CHRISTIANS

Many important elements are common between Islam and Christianity Muslims and Christians share many similar beliefs, values, moral injunctions and principles of behavior The fundamental difference between the two faiths concerns the nature and role of Jesus.

In Islam, Jesus the Messiah (God's peace and blessings be on him) is one of the greatest of the prophets whom Muslims love and hold in very deep respect. The Quran confirms that Jesus was born of a virgin mother (Maryam) through the same Power which brought Adam into being without a father, and that by God's permission during his prophethood he wrought many compelling miracles among his people. He was given the power to speak coherently in infancy, to heal the sick, to raise the dead, and to reach the hearts of men by the words which God revealed to him. Finally, when he was in danger of being killed by his own people, God raised him up to himself without his experiencing death (Holy Quran 4:157-158 and 3:55).[55] We cite here some passages from the Quran relating to Jesus' life and mission:

> *"Behold, the angels said, 'O Mary! Lo, God gives thee glad tidings of a word from Him, whose name is the Messiah Jesus, son of Mary, illustrious in the world and the hereafter and one of those brought near (unto God). He will speak to men in his cradle and in his manhood, and he will be of the righteous.' She said, 'My Lord! How can I have a child when no man has touched me.' He (the angel) said, 'Thus God creates what He wills. If He decrees a thing, He says unto it only "Be," and it is.' And He will teach him the Scripture and the wisdom and the Torah and the Injeel.[56] And He will make him a messenger to the Children of Israel, (saying) "Lo, I come to you with a sign from your Lord. Lo, I fashion for you out of clay the likeness of a bird and I breathe into it and it is a bird by God's leave. I heal him who was born blind and the leper and I raise the dead by God's lease. And I announce to you what you eat and what you store up in your houses. Lo! herein verily is a sign for you if you are indeed believers. And (I come) confirming that which was before me of the Torah, and to make lawful some of that which was forbidden to you I come to you with a sign from your Lord so keep your duty to God and obey me. Verily, God is my Lord and your Lord so worship Him That is a straight path."'"(3:45-51)*

*"Verily! the likeness of Jesus with God is as the likeness
of Adam He created him of dust then He said unto him 'Be,'
and he was." (3:59)*

*". . . . and for their saying, 'We killed the Messiah Jesus son
of Mary, God's Messenger,' they did not kill him nor did they
crucify him but it appeared so to them; and indeed, those who
disagree concerning it are in doubt about it. They have no
knowledge concerning it except the pursuit of a conjecture and
assuredly they did not kill him. Nay, God raised him up unto
Himself And God is Mighty Wise." (4:157-158)*

Then what about Christianity's claim that Jesus is the son of
God? In order to answer this question we must deal with two fundamental issues (1) Could the Exalted Creator and Lord of the
universe in fact have a son, and (2) is it possible that Jesus himself could have claimed and actually did claim to be God's son?

We note that although the Quran confirms that Jesus was
born without the agency of a father, this simply means that God,
Who establishes the regularity of functioning of natural phenomena which we understand as natural laws, is equally able to sus-
pend them when it pleases Him that is, He is able to create what
He wills when, how and as He chooses. It does not make Jesus
God's progeny or in any way a sharer in His divine nature any
more than it does Adam, who was also created without a father
and likewise without a mother. The Quran states emphatically in
passage after passage that Jesus is not God's son; that he never
claimed to be God's son or of divine nature but rather charged his
followers to worship God alone; and that the notion of the Most
High God's having a son is so totally degrading to and far
removed from the exaltedness and transcendence of God's divine
nature that it actually constitutes an awesome piece of blasphemy. The Quran says concerning this:

*"And they say, 'The Merciful has taken unto Himself a
son.' Assuredly you utter a disastrous thing at which the heavens are almost torn and the earth is split asunder and the
mountains fall into ruins because you ascribe to the Merciful*

a son when it is not befitting for (the majesty) of the Merciful that He should take a son. There is none in the heavens and the earth but comes to the Merciful as a servant." (19:88-93)

For the Creator and Sustainer of this infinitely complex and vast universe is far above anything we can conceive of, and the physical attributes and limitations of created beings can never be imagined to apply to Him. If Jesus were indeed God's son, he would be a sharer in the Godhead and of divine nature himself, and in that case God would have simultaneously begotten, been begotten, been born, lived as a human being and died. Such a notion does not merit any comment. It has much more in common with pagan mythologies, in which gods fathered semi-divine children by human women than with a true religion coming from God and based on the reality of the relationship between the Creator and the created. Hence the claim that Jesus is God's son cannot be, by its very nature, other than a false one because it contradicts the very nature and attributes of the Creator Himself, bringing Him down to the level of the beings He has created. In the words of the Quran:

"They say, 'God has begotten a son.' Glory be to Him! Nay to Him belongs all that is in the heavens and on earth. Everything renders worship to Him. To Him is due the primal origin of the heavens and the earth. When He decrees a matter He (merely) says to it, "Be," and it is."' (2:116-117)

We now turn to the second question whether Jesus himself (peace be on him) could possibly have claimed to be God's son. The answer is very obvious; that he could not and did not do so is clear from the nature of the Message he brought. Can it possibly make the slightest sense that God divides up His unique and indivisible nature between Himself and His son, and that the son commands people to worship him instead of his father? This clearly means two gods rather than One God, the dividing of what is indivisible, and the splitting up of the power, authority and rule in the universe. Hence one is forced to conclude that the claim that Jesus is the son of God could not possibly have been made by him but was made on his behalf and in his name without his knowledge and/or consent by some other person. We cite here some Quranic passages concerning the nature of Jesus (peace be on him) and the Message he brought. These and many other references to these subjects recur over and over in many different parts of the Quran.

"O People of the Book! Do not exaggerate in your religion nor utter anything concerning God except the truth. Verily! the Messiah, Jesus the son of Mary was only a messenger of God and His Word which He conveyed unto Mary and a soul from Him. So believe in God and His messengers, and do not say, 'Three,' (the Trinity). Cease! It is better for you! God is only One God. It is far removed from His transcendent majesty that He should have a son. His is all that is in the heavens and all that is in the earth. And God is sufficient as a Protector. The Messiah would never scorn to be a slave to God, nor would the favored angels . . ." (4:171-172)

"They indeed disbelieve who say, 'Lo, God is the Messiah, the son of Mary.' Say: 'Who then could do anything against God if He had willed to destroy the Messiah, the son of Mary, and his mother and everyone on earth?' God's is the sovereignty in the heavens and the earth and all that is between them. He creates what He wills. And God has power over all things.'" (5:17-19)

"They indeed disbelieve who say, 'Lo, God is the Messiah, the son of Mary.' The Messiah (himself) said: 'O Children of Israel. worship God, my Lord and your Lord.' Verily, whoever ascribes partners to God, God has forbidden him the garden. His abode is the fire. And for the evil-doers there will be no helpers. They indeed disbelieve who say, 'Lo, God is the third of three,' when there is no deity except the One God. If they do not desist from saying so, a painful punishment will fall on those of them who disbelieve. . . . The Messiah, the son of Mary, was no more than a messenger, messengers (the like of whom) had passed away before him, and his mother

was a devout woman, and they both ate food.[53] *See how We make clear to them Our signs, yet see how they are turned away."* (5:72/75-73, 76, 75/78)

"And behold, God will say (on the day of judgment), 'O Jesus son of Mary! Did you say to people, "Take me and my mother as deities besides God?"' He will say, 'Glory be to You! It was not for me to say that for which I had no right . . . I said to them only what You did command me: "Worship God. my Lord and Your Lord."'" (5:116- 119)

"Verily, he (Jesus) was nothing except a slave upon whom We bestowed favor and made an example for the Children of Israel.... And when Jesus came with clear proofs, he said, 'I have come to you with wisdom, and to make plain some of that concerning which you differ. So remain conscious of God and obey me. Verily, God is my Lord and your Lord. That is the straight path.'" (43:59 63-64)

"It is not for any human being to whom God has given the Book (a revealed scripture) and the wisdom and the prophethood that he should then say to people, 'Be servants of me instead of God.' but rather, 'Be faithful servants of the Lord, for you have taught the Book and you have studied it earnestly.'" (3:79)

"And behold, Jesus the son of Mary said. 'O Children of Israel! Lo, I am the Messenger of God to you, confirming that which was (revealed) before me in the Torah and bringing good tidings of a messenger who comes after me whose name is Ahmad . . .'" (61:6)[58]

If one drops any mention of "the son of God" from the New Testament accounts of the life of Jesus (peace be on him), it becomes clear that he must in truth have been a prophet in the line of the other prophets raised among the Children of Israel who, like his predecessors, brought a revelation or scripture addressed to them by God. It is therefore impossible that this revelation could have been a new religion centering around Jesus himself; for one who was commissioned by God the All-Knowing, to convey His guidance and call people to submit to Him, could never have claimed sonship or divinity something which no one possesses or asked people to worship him instead of or in addition to God Jesus himself strictly adhered to the Law brought by Moses (peace be on him), and his mission was to revive and confirm the divine guidance which Moses and the prophets who followed had brought, not to establish a new religion.

The Scripture revealed through him therefore addressed itself to the contemporary situation of the Children of Israel, insisting that the earlier Scripture was binding upon them and must be followed but with sincerity, inner piety and true God-consciousness rather than with empty ritual and insincere show of devoutness. Those whom God loves, Jesus taught, who will inherit His Kingdom, are not the inwardly-empty official men of religion but those who love God, obey His guidance with fear and awe in their hearts, and surrender themselves to Him. These are chiefly to be found among the ordinary people, often the simple and humble who are held to be of no account in the eyes of the world although their hearts are sincere and true to their Lord, instead of among the proud and status-conscious.

But if Jesus did not himself say that he was the son of God and savior of the world, how is it that the Gospels attribute such a claim to him? And how is it that all Christians since his time have believed this?

First of all, not all Christians, even at the present time, believe this. Some groups exist today which do not believe in his divinity and in early times there were a number of sects, later pronounced to be heretical when it was "decided" that Jesus was of divine nature who differed on this matter, holding that Jesus was a human being and a prophet; among them were some which did not believe that Jesus was crucified but that another person very much resembling him was crucified in his stead.[59] Such sects were suppressed and almost entirely obliterated. The

American Muslim scholar Sulaiman Mufassir writes: "*It is significant that those doctrines which the Quran affirms can be easily proven to be part of the teachings of the early disciples, whereas those doctrines which the Quran rejects prove to be later Church additions, inspired by the philosophies and cults of pagan Greece and Rome.*" (italics Mufassir's).[59]

As to the claim attributed to Jesus (peace be on him) of being God's son, it must be remembered that the four New Testament Gospels, the books of Matthews, Marks, Luke, and John were written many years after Jesus' time. Biblical scholarship has established the fact that none of their authors was the immediate disciple of Jesus; moreover, they did not write in Jesus' own language Aramaic, but in Greek. By the time they wrote their accounts of his life, a great many things about Jesus had been lost or forgotten and many more had been interpolated and moreover Christianity was by then being molded into a form which would appeal to Greeks and Romans rather than to Palestinian Jews.

Now let us suppose that an individual of some note or fame were to live among us carry on his work and depart or die. Can we suppose that an account of his life written initially as long as forty years after his death would be really accurate especially if he had lived in a community in which writing detailed accounts concerning people was not common? And if he later grew into a public figure, something of a legend, we could be very certain that the narrative would in addition be considerably embellished by people's imaginations, and that at the same time a wealth of very important details would have been lost. The account would moreover be colored by the understandings of the writers and would unquestionable reflect their own views and ideas concerning the person they were describing.

The accounts of the four Gospels are analogous to such a situation. Jesus (God's peace and blessings be on him) most certainly did bring a divinely-revealed scripture. However, although it is obvious from their content that the four Gospels do contain some parts of the message of submission and accountability which Jesus brought, these are simply biographical accounts of Jesus' life and mission by four different men not the divine revelation brought by Jesus itself. The greater part of the material contained in the four Gospels does not meet the criteria discussed earlier by which a true revelation may be recognized, the first of which is that it should be transmitted word for word as received from God by the person to whom it was directly revealed not through a second- or fifth-hand source. Even the claim that the Gospels were written under divine inspiration does not hold together since there are many inconsistencies and discrepancies among these four equally "inspired" accounts.

Without doubt, what Jesus (peace be on him) actually claimed was not that he was the son of God (an incredible piece of blasphemy from the mouth of a devout and committed follower of the teachings of the prophets), but that he was the Messiah, a prophet in the line of the previous messengers of God, and that He received a divine Scripture from Him. But it is apparent that the message brought by Jesus, the message to the Children of Israel concerning their accountability to God and their obligation to follow the guidance revealed through Prophet Moses (peace be on him), was later changed, taken out of its pure monotheistic context, and made to conform to the pagan Hellenistic conceptions of the time; this was done to render it more attractive to the Greeks and Romans among whom it was being propagated, who would never have been impressed with the pure, simple message of submission to a non-corporeal, transcendent Deity which Jesus in fact proclaimed. That this Message was intended solely for the Jews and that it insisted on adherence to the Mosaic Law was completely lost sight of in this attempt to gain converts throughout the pagan Roman Empire.

The conclusion to be drawn from all this is that although in the four Gospels of the New Testament we can find obvious traces of the message which Jesus (peace be on him) brought in his emphasis on the human being's accountability to God, the necessity of sincerity and obedience to Him, and the certainty of the day of judgment and the hereafter, the claim attributed to Jesus of being the son of God is so completely at variance not only with the Oneness and Uniqueness of God Most High but also with the remainder of the message of submission to God which Jesus brought that it is impossible to regard it as other than a fabrication. This fits in with the fact that later Christianity was abundantly interwoven with mythological content drawn heavily from pagan sources, plus a theology which was produced as the need arose to suit the mentality of the times and protect the hold of a power-hungry priesthood over the masses.

Then what about the belief that the human being is saved from eternal damnation by accepting Jesus as his savior? The notion of original sin is one which Islam emphatically denies, affirming that every human being comes into the world innocent and sinless. Accordingly, he will be held accountable only for what he himself inscribes upon the unblemished *tabula rasa* of his nature, not for what his ancestor Adam[60] (or anyone else whomsoever) did or did not do. For each human individual is responsible only for his own actions; neither sin nor righteousness are "hereditary" characteristics which can be transferred from one person to another or which are carried in the "blood" or "nature" of human beings. The Quran emphasizes this again and again:

> *"No soul earns (anything) but against itself, and no bear-er of burdens shall bear the burden of another."* (6:164)

> *". . . that no burdened one shall bear another's burden, and that man will have only that for which he makes an effort and that his effort will be seen, and that afterwards he will be repaid for it with fullest repayment, and that verily to your Lord is the goal."* (53:38-42)

> *"And fear a day when no soul will avail another in anything, nor will compensation be accepted from it nor will intercession profit it nor will anyone be helped."* (2:123)

Hence, to attribute to God, the Forgiving and Merciful, His laying upon each new-born infant the intolerable burden of a sin committed by his remotest ancestor would appear to be a denial of His unquestionable attributes of justice, mercy, kindness and compassion toward His creatures. And to further claim that the taint of this sin is certain to put every human being into hell for all eternity unless the deity sacrifices Himself for His creatures whom He is able to, and should if He is indeed Just and Merciful, forgive, is a denial not only of His unfailing justice and good-will toward His creation but also, it would seem, of His wisdom, logic and reasonableness. Islam emphatically proclaims that no one can be saved from hell by any means except the mercy and grace of God, contingent upon his acknowledging God as his Lord, surrendering his whole being to Him and following the guidance which He has revealed. The loving and merciful God is able to and does forgive sins if repentance is sincere, and every human soul has direct access to its Source and to His forgiveness without any intermediary or intercessor whatever. Consequently there is no need for a savior, and in any case God Most High alone can save.

Another major point of difference between Islam and Christianity is in the doctrine of the trinity. If God is One, as Christians profess to believe just as Muslims do, there is no way by which He can at the same time be three; even a very young child can grasp the obvious truth of this. The trinity is usually explained by Christians as meaning not three gods but three parts or persons of the One God having different functions. But God is not like a pie or an apple which can be divided into three thirds which form one whole; if God is three persons or possesses three parts, He is assuredly not the Single, Unique, Indivisible Being which God is and which Christianity professes to believe in. To Muslims this makes absolutely no sense, and even if it is explained as being a "mystery" too high for any human mind to grasp, belief in the trinity is regarded by Islam, as we have seen in the Quranic verses just cited, as a form of polytheism. For all these reasons, Muslims hold that they themselves are much closer to the teachings of Jesus (God's peace and blessings be on him) than is the Christianity of the Church which, they feel, has tampered with and distorted the Message which the Holy Messenger Jesus brought by ascribing divinity to him.

Such differences in viewpoint, however, should not be taken

as grounds for antagonism or heated theological arguments between Muslims and Christians The Quran admonishes:

> *"And do not dispute with the People of the Scripture unless it be in (a way) which is better, except with those of them who are wrongdoers and says 'We believe in that which has been revealed to us and revealed to your and our God and your God is one, and unto Him do we submit.'"* (29:46)

For what is common between the followers of the two faiths is many basic beliefs and the vast legacy of moral injunctions and principles of behavior inspired by belief in the same God and the guidance conveyed by Jesus (peace be on him), which should inspire in them friendship, sympathy and appreciation for the others' sincerity simply "agreeing to disagree" on their differences. In the words of the Quran:

> *". . . Say (O Muhammad): 'I have submitted my will to God and (so have) those who follow me.' And say to those who have received the Scripture and to those who do not read, 'Have you submitted?' Then if they submit, truly they are rightly-guided and if they turn away, then it is thy duty only to convey the message. And in God's sight are all His servants."* (3:20)

Assuredly, in the face of the almost overwhelming array of problems and evils in the world today, the true believers in God have an obligation to put aside their differences and make common cause as believers in the fight against atheism, disregard for God's laws and every kind of wrongdoing. This struggle is a duty for them all, one in which they should support and reinforce each other. As the number of indigenous and immigrant Muslims continues to increase in the Western world, it is hoped that they will make very significant contributions to the societies in which they live, side by side with other like-minded people, by making Islam's point of view known and drawing upon the vast legacy of its teachings to work toward solutions of the many grave problems and dilemmas confronting mankind.

PART FIVE: CONCLUSION

What we have presented here has been a very brief glimpse, a small window, as it were, looking into an exceedingly vast and complex subject. Indeed, the body of Islamic knowledge and exposition, concerned with every facet of beliefs, worship, values, morals and behavior, both individual and collective, is so immense that scholars have spent entire lifetimes to master some part of this knowledge without being able to contain it all.

But what we have been talking about all through this book, and what that vast reservoir of Islamic knowledge is all about, can readily be summed up in one brief word: submission. The aim and direction of all of it is to help the human individual, in his inward and outward aspects, his physical being as well as his mind and soul, his collective as well as his personal concerns, to live a life which is surrendered, by will and by deed, to God Most High.

For human beings, due to their very nature, need, want and in fact do submit to something. The only relevant question then is, to whom or what? To be a Muslim is to answer this most fundamental of all the questions facing a human individual by submitting one's life to God the Praised and Exalted alone, following the guidance of Islam, which consists, in essence, of the instructions of the Lord of the universe to His creatures, all the human individuals of this world both past and present, concerning how to submit to Him.

> *"Say: 'Verily, my prayer and my worship, my life and my death, are for God, the Lord of the worlds. He has no associate. This I am commanded, and I am the first of those who submit.'"* (6:162-163)

211

NOTES

1 Even when, during the course of history, human beings have wandered away from belief in God as the sole Sustainer and Controller of all that exists, they have not as a rule denied the fact of His *existence*. Rather they have invented associates or partners in His divinity, ascribing some part of His powers to them while simultaneously acknowledging His supremacy over them.

2 The articles of faith are not in any fixed sequential order because they are independent and simultaneous principles. Hence they may appear in different orders in various presentations of Islam.

3 Yet another species of intelligent beings are *jinn* who, the Quran tells us, are made from fire. Like the human being, they possess freedom of choice. Some of them are good and others are evil. According to Islam, satan (iblis) and his kind are *jinn* (not fallen angels) to whom God gave leave to try to tempt the human being, to lure him away from submission and obedience to Him. Thus the human being must strive throughout his life against *"the evil of the whisperer who withdraws, the one who whispers into the hearts of mankind from among jinn and among men."* (114:4-6) The Quran makes it clear that one whose life is centered on God can easily repel satan, whose strategy is weak, while one who is in a state of denial or rebellion against God is likely to be in satan's grip, the prey of evil within himself and without.

4 The single known exception to this is the Prophet Moses to whom God spoke directly.

5 Gabriel is referred to in the Quran as *ar-rooh* (the Spirit), *rooh al-qudus* (the Holy Spirit) and *rooh al-ameen* (the Trustworthy Spirit). It is possible that through some error of understanding the early Christians may mistakenly have taken the angel Gabriel to be part of the Godhead under the influence of the pagan conceptions surrounding them, considering him as the Holy Spirit to be the third person of the trinity (see Quran 2:253, in which we read: *"And We gave Jesus, son of Mary, clear evidences and We aided him with the Holy Spirit,"* [*rooh al-qudus*, referring to Gabriel]).

6 God speaks of Himself in the Quran interchangeably as I, He and We.

7 The original scripture revealed to Jesus.

8 The original scripture revealed to Moses.

9 It is perhaps very difficult for many of us, in this age of loss of spiritual values and lack of spiritual individuals, to imagine or even believe in the possibility of a human being good enough to be a prophet. Yet even today among the devout Muslims, there do exist individuals who are so absolutely pure in heart and in conduct, so deep in faith and so near to God that although they are still far from approaching the character of a prophet, they nevertheless make it possible to understand that such a person, totally surrendered to God and submitting to Him with the entirety of his being, could and in fact did actually exist.

10 An exception to this is the translation of A. J. Arberry. A list of the better translations will be found among the list of suggested reading at the end of this volume.

11 For an elaboration of this see *The Bible, Quran and Science* by Maurice Bucaille available at KAZI Publications.

12 See Abdul Hameed Siddiqui, *The Life of Muhammad*, KAZI Publications, Chicago, 1975, pp 59-63 for a discussion of this point.

13 Islam holds that a prophet possesses the following characteristics: he is absolutely truthful; he is free of any kind of major sins; he delivers the message with which he has been charged without any failure or concealment; and he is of the highest order of intelligence and mental ability. Obviously if those who claim prophethood do not possess such essential qualities, Almighty God can be accused of ineptitude in His selection of the people to whom He has entrusted the most important task on earth!

14 An alternative wording used interchangeably with the above is "*wa ashaduanna Muhammadan abduhu wa rasooluhu*" ". . . .and I bear witness that Muhammad is His servant and messenger"). This denotes that even Muhammad, the best and most perfect of all men, was, like all other human beings, God's humble servant. This makes it clear that the terms servant and messenger are complementary, not contradictory, because the greatest of prophets is, in spite of his exalted station among his fellow human beings, just as much as the humblest of men or the worst of sinners, God's servant, albeit the most honored among all the servants of God.

15 As stated previously, Muslims always recite the Quran in Arabic during *salah*, whether they are Arabic-speaking or not. A new convert to Islam who does not know Arabic may recite verses in translation in his/her own language until able to memorize at least two short passages in Arabic which is generally fairly easy for most people to do.

16 This refers to converts to Islam who are in material difficulties for one reason or another after embracing Islam.

17 The ancient name for Mecca.

18 On the following day, Muslims throughout the world observe one of Islam's two major feasts, the Festival of Sacrifice (*eid al-adha*). On this occasion it is *sunnah* to slaughter an animal (which is also one of the observances of *hajj*) in commemoration of Prophet Abraham's sacrifice of a sheep in place of his son.

19 Although the Old Testament (Genesis 22:1-2) refers to Isaac as the object of the intended sacrifice, the error in this account is made clear by the fact that it refers to Isaac or Abraham's "only son," when it is an historic fact that his son Ishmael, according to the Bible, was born thirteen years before his son Isaac.

20 The Kabah is approximately 45 feet high, 33 feet wide and 50 feet long.

21 This refers to a spot adjacent to the Kabah where Abraham worshiped.

22 Although the central purpose of the Kabah was always acknowledged to be the worship of God, for a time, beginning long before the birth of Prophet Muhammad, it was the center of the idolatrous worship of the pagan Arabs. Inside it stood a vast number of idols which were worshiped together with God. When the Prophet gained the final victory over the Meccans, he demolished the idols and the Kabah was again restored to its original sacred purpose, that of worship of Almighty God alone.

23 Many people think, incorrectly, that Muslims always face "the East" when they pray. In fact, they face the direction of the Kabah wherever it may lie from the place in which they are. In most of the United States and Canada, this direction is north-east. Although this might appear strange at first glance, if a string is stretched over a globe, it will be readily apparent that the shortest distance from most of North America to Mecca is in a north-easterly direction rather than south-easterly as one might suppose.

24 The number of worshippers in the Sacred Mosque of course depends upon the season. During *hajj* it accommodates hundreds of thousands of Muslims. On other occasions, for example, during Ramadan, on the two festivals and on Fridays, it is also very crowded while at other times the numbers are far less.

25 Islamic tradition holds that Abraham brought his wife Hagar and son Ishmael to the barren valley of Mecca, then a desolate, uninhabited spot surrounded by stark lava hills and left them there at God's command. When their supply of water was exhausted and the child began to cry with thirst, Hagar began a hurried search for water, running back and forth seven times between two small hillocks. Her search proved futile, but when she turned back to her son, God revealed to her the spring of Zamzam flowing at his feet. It has flowed continuously since that time. The presence of water in the midst of the inhospitable desert attracted settlers to the spot which in time became the city of Mecca. In later years Abraham together with his son Ishmael built the Kabah very close to the spring.

26 The Quran repeatedly appeals to human beings to use their reason to discover for themselves the undeniable evidences of this Power in the natural world, citing such examples as the alternation of night and day, the orbiting of the heavenly bodies, the earth and its geographic features, the multi-faceted uses of animals for men, man's own existence and his progress from state to state, the flight of birds, trees and fruits and crops, the oceans with their treasures and their utility to human beings and many others.

27 See footnote 14 for an elaboration of the significance of the concept of man's servanthood to God in relation to the Holy Prophet's being, no less than any other human being of any status, God's humble servant.

28 These are the words with which a believer receives the news of a death of any calamity.

29 For example, *insh* Allah (if God wills), *ma'sh* Allah (as God has willed it), *subhan* Allah (glory be to God), *al-hamd* Allah (praise be to God), *astaghfir* Allah (may God forgive), *jazak* Allah *al-khayr* (may God reward you with good), and many others.

30 A word needs to be said here about the terms Sunni and Shi'ah. These denote groupings within the community of Islam based not on differences in fundamentals of belief but rather on the concept of successorship to the Prophet (peace be on him). Sunnis hold that the Prophet did not designate anyone to succeed him as the leader and head of the Muslim *ummah* and state after his death, and thus the first four caliphs were rightfully chosen from among the people, while Shi'ahs hold that the Prophet designated Ali, his cousin and son-in-law, as his successor, and that the leader of the *ummah* should be from among the Prophet's descendants through Ali and his wife Fatimah, the daughter of the Prophet. Although the differences of view point between Shi'ahs and Sunnis have been widely publicized, within the mainstream of Shi'ah thought, they do not concern basic conceptions, teachings or practices and are on the whole relatively minor in nature.

31 Here the Prophet's own example is instructive and inspiring. He was married to one woman, his first wife, Khadijah, for twenty-five years, living with her in the greatest harmony and tenderness. Only after her death, after he reached the age of fifty, did he contract other marriages, each one to cement friendships, promote alliances or teach some essential lesson to his community, and to provide a vital example to Muslims of how to treat one's spouses under the varied conditions of life.

32 This is the first fundamental principle for the conduct of government in Islam, that of obedience to the *ameer* (the leader or head of state).

33 The second principle is that of *shura* or mutual consultation between the *ameer* and the people.

34 Islam does not lay down a particular method for the selection of the leader. However, his selection by the consent of the people and the evidence of their willingness to follow his leadership, are fundamental principles.

35 While such punishments as the execution of those who commit premeditat-

ed murder or robbery with murder, cutting off the fingers or hand of a habitu-
al thief (this excludes those who steal due to poverty), the stoning of adulter-
ers (only after guilt has been unquestionably established in court by four eye-
witnesses to the act or by self-confession, which means in effect that the punishment is virtually never carried out), or the public lashing of fornicators or
drinkers may seem harsh to many people who are accustomed to living in
societies in which such violations of moral codes are so common as to be
taken as a normal and necessary condition of life, the Islamic view is that
these constitute very serious and criminal offenses against morality and the
social order, and are neither necessary nor to be tolerated. Hence the Islamic
punishments, called in Arabic *hudood*, that is, the limits imposed by God, are
not in fact intended merely as penalties for a proven crime but as deterrents
against further crime. As a result, in those societies in which the punishments
prescribed by the Islamic *shariah* are enforced, there is little or no crime, and
citizens feel safe, protected by a law so strict that virtually no one dares to
risk transgressing it. To those who argue that such penalties are harsh and do
not show compassion to criminals, Islam's answer is that the criminal's own
lack of compassion in violating an innocent victim has forfeited him the right
to be treated indulgently by society. It sees failure to administer adequate punishments to violators of moral codes as the ultimate injustice to the people of
the society. That in many places people cannot walk alone in the streets due to
fear of rape or robbery, and that they cannot feel safe even in securely locked
houses, may be very fair to criminals but it is assuredly not fair to those who
live in constant fear of attack. Crime is to be dealt with at its source by elimi-
nating the problems which lead people to it, whether these are lack of a sense
of responsibility to God and to other human beings, emotional insecurity, economic frustrations, injustice, etc., rather than by encouraging crime through
failure to provide adequate deterrents. See the leading article, "Moslem
Justice," *Wall Street Journal*, May 11, 1979.

36 The fact that there are many places in the Muslim world today where small
groups of non-Muslims live and carry on their religious practices and traditions without hindrance in the midst of the Muslim majority should be sufficient proof that "conversion by the sword" is a fiction, for Islam strictly prohibits forced conversions. An additional proof to which history bears witness
is the fact that on occasion Muslim armies were welcomed with joy and relief
by non-Muslim people living under oppressive rulers, who knew that
Muslims, although professing a different faith, would govern them with a tolerance and justice which they often could not obtain from their own co-reli-
gionists.

37 The penalty for *deliberate* failure to fast on any day of Ramadan except for

the above valid reasons is fasting for sixty consecutive days for *every* day so missed, or, if one is unable to do this, to spend in charity an amount equivalent to feeding sixty persons for each missed day. The same very stringent penalty applies for any day on which one interrupts his fast intentionally without a valid reason. However, if one eats or drinks unintentionally, forgetting that he is fasting, there is no penalty since the mistake was not deliberate.
38 This is why Muslims—that is, "those who submit to God"—strongly object to being called Muhammedans, i.e., followers of the man Muhammad.
39 Near male blood relatives with whom Islam prohibits marriage, e.g., father, son, brother, grandfather, uncle, nephew, as well as father-in-law and brother through suckling the same nurse in infancy and mahram to a woman and the corresponding female relatives are *mahram* to a man.
40 That is, take care to maintain and strengthen the ties of blood relationship.
41 Their husbands' rights to sexual exclusiveness, his honor and his property.
42 The two women whom the Quran holds up as models of virtue (66:11-12) are the wife of the tyrannical pharaoh of Moses' time who, in spite of her husband's power and oppressive behavior, kept herself aloof from all evil, taking refuge in God from his wickedness, and Mary, the mother of Jesus, a pure and devout woman. Both of these were women of immense spirituality and nobility. Like them, the three greatest women of early Islamic times—Khadijah, the Prophet's first wife whom he loved so devotedly, Aisha, the quick-minded young wife of his later years, and Fatimah, his patient, devout daughter—were examples of intelligence, deep spirituality and many other good qualities.
43 If men and women are held to be equal in Islam, why does it appear to favor men in such matters as inheritance (which stipulates that the share of the male is as a rule twice that of the female) and legal evidence (the testimony of two females being equal to that of one male), it may be asked? Although these two matters appear to concern the same issue, in fact they involve two totally unrelated situations. Let us examine them one by one.

As we have seen, in Islam the responsibility for the maintenance of women falls upon men. A woman's earnings, property or inheritance is unqualifiedly hers to keep and to use as she wishes; even if she has money, she is not obliged to use it for her own maintenance or to support her children or husband. It will thus be readily apparent that since man bears the economic burden of the support of women, it is only just that his share of inheritance should be more than that of a woman, who is free to spend her money in any way she pleases.

Concerning the question of the witness of two women being equal to that of one man, so that "*if (as the Quran says) one makes a mistake the other can remind her*" (2:292). These provisions have been made to safeguard the rights of the accused, for in Islam an individual is innocent unless proved guilty and it is considered more desirable to withhold punishment from a guilty person than to erroneously punish someone who is innocent.

44 At the same time, Islam, which is for people of all levels and conditions, recognizes the fact that some women, those who are difficult, unresponsive or incapable of mature behavior, do not always respond to good treatment. Hence men are permitted to show their displeasure to such recalcitrant wives by first, a verbal admonition, then leaving their beds and finally a token beating. But this, by the Prophet's own order, is to be of such a mild nature that it does not hurt or inflict harm but rather serves to show a woman who cannot be reached by other means that the situation is a now serious. In no case is verbal or physical abuse which hurts, harms or humiliated one's wife permitted by Islam.

45 Islam does not include cousins within the circle of *mahram* relationships. Hence cousin marriage is permitted and is very common in the Muslim world.

46 Not to look very directly or with interest or sexual intent at the opposite sex.

47 Islam does not require men to wear a particular type of dress but it does require that their dress be modest. As we are all aware, any dress can be worn either in a modest manner or in a manner which betrays other motives.

48 All alcoholic drinks and alcohol-containing flavors such as pure vanilla and other extracts are to be avoided. This also constitutes a problem in regard to medicines and other items such as mouth wash which contain alcohol.

49 Lard and unspecified animal fat are to be avoided since many commercial fats are mixtures of pork fat and other fats.

50 Gelatin is ordinarily made from beef bones and animal hide trimmings, especially those of swine. Gelatin is found in gelatin desserts and salads, marshmallows, some cream pies, cake fillings, candies, commercial yogurt and other foods. Kosher gelatin may also be of pork origin because many Jews consider gelatin to be a chemical and not an animal ingredient.

51 That is, the face and hands and whatever shows by accident, i.e., due to wind blowing the garments, etc.

52 We often tend to forget that modern Western dress is a very new inventions; as recently as seventy years ago, all Western women wore a dress similar to the Islamic modest dress. People who imagine that the Islamic dress of women in impractical and interferes with activity have lost sight of how active and hard-working women of other times, for example, pioneer women, were in spite of their long, full dresses and various types of head coverings.

53 Many people wonder about "the veil." The word "veil" has been used in the Western media to mean both a head covering (which Islam requires) and the covering of the face. Veiling the face is common in many Muslim countries, either with a full covering or a partial one which leaves the eyes and forehead exposed. Today many sincere and committed Muslim women veil their faces out of the conviction that Islam requires it or that it is best. Many others, however, veil their faces as a mere societal tradition rather than an Islamic requirement and while the face may be nominally covered, the remaining requirements of *hijab* are often neglected. Is veiling the face an Islamic requirement? A small minority of Islamic scholars hold that covering the face is required, while the majority are of the opinion that it is not necessary or required by Islam.

54 Only two examples of this may be mentioned here. One is the account of creation (Genesis, Chapter 1), in which God first creates light and then the earth with its oceans and dry land, vegetation, etc., and after this, on the *third* day of creation, He creates the sun and moon. On the seventh day, He is so weary from His labor that He must rest. Again, in Deuteronomy 34:5-7, in an account which is supposed to have been written by Moses himself, we read about the death and burial of Moses. The whole of the Old Testament is interspersed with such serious inconsistencies and inaccuracies that it is clear that it cannot be the original scripture revealed by God to Moses and the other prophets, although parts of it—what parts is not clear, apart from, undoubtedly, the Ten Commandments—may have been preserved in it.

55 *The Gospel of Barnabas* (see Suggested Reading) speaks eloquently of this matter.

56 The Injeel (Evangel or Good News) is the original scripture revealed to Jesus by God. This is not, however, to be confused with the New Testament Gospels. See the discussion that follows.

57 That is, they required sustenance for their existence like any other created beings, proving that they were of human, not divine, nature.

58 The Arabic names Ahmad and Muhammad are both derived from the same root letters *h-m-d* which mean "praise," and both have the same meaning: the Praised One. Thus Prophet Muhammad is often referred to as Ahmad. It is also to be noted that the coming of Muhammad, the prophet raised from among "the brethren" of the Children of Israel, may be what was prophesied in Deuteronomy 18:15, 18-19, and in Acts 3:22. See also *The Gospel of Barnabas*.

59 *Ibid.*, p. 14.

60 It is to be remembered that Islam teaches that the first man, Adam, was also the first prophet to whom God gave guidance for himself and his descendants after he disobeyed God and, turning to Him in repentance for his sin, was forgiven.

SUGGESTED READING

Athar, Alia, *Prophets: Models for Humanity*. Moving beyond the traditional story-like style, the author in this pioneering work elucidates the lives of the prophets in the context of their continuing struggle between good and evil. Based on the Quran and the *sunnah*, the lives of thirty prophets unfold for the reader.

Bakhtiar, Laleh, *Encyclopedia of Islamic Law: A Compendium of the Major Schools*. The Hanafi, Hanbali, Shafii, Maliki and Jafari schools of Islamic law are compared and contrasted on issues of Islamic law including marriage, divorce, prayer, fasting, pilgrimage, and so forth.

Bakhtiar, Laleh, *Muhammad's Companions. Essays on Some Who Bore Witness to His Message*. In an exciting and lucid way, this work tells of the interaction of the life of the Messenger with the lives of thirty-three Companions, thirteen of whom are women. Those people are blessed with being able to participate in the Islamic movement in its making.

Bakhtiar, Laleh (ed.), *Ramadan: Motivating Muslims to Action: An Interfaith Perspective*. Ramadan is not just a month of fasting, but a month of spiritual healing. Presented from an interfaith perspective as a means to motivate believers to action, the articles by such famous writers as Muhammad al-Ghazzali, Shaykh Abdul Qadir Gilani, Imam Jawziyya, Ibn Sireen, Seyyed Hossein Nasr, Maulana Mawdudi and Laleh Bakhtiar include essays on both the Law and the Way.

Bakhtiar, Laleh, *Sufi Women of America: Angels in the Making*. A compelling report of the lives of seven women who first accepted submission to God's Will and then commitment to inner change as their way of life.

_____*The Holy Quran*. Translations recommended include those by Marmaduke Pickthall, Abdullah Yusuf Ali (available in paperback), A. J. Arberry, and Abul Ala Maududi. Due to the difficulties in translating the sublime language and rhythms of the Quran, none of these translations can be considered very adequate, but they are the best available to date. Pickthall's and Arberry's translations are without commentary. Yusuf Ali has an extensive commentary but it is not scholarly or very adequate, while Maududi's is an excellent, detailed and very scholarly explanation of the meaning of the Quran.

Hughes, Patrick, *Dictionary of Islam*. This is the only comprehensive, fully illustrated *Dictionary of Islam* available in English in one volume. It is an encyclopedia of the doctrines, rites, ceremonies, and customs together with the technical and theological terms of the Islamic faith. Written in the 19th century and reprinted in this beautiful US Edition, it is a handy reference.

Nasr, Seyyed Hossein, *A Young Muslim's Guide to the Modern World*. This guide for the Muslim to the modern world—the first of its kind in any language—presents the eternal truths of Islam as well as Western religious and intellectual tradition as they confront each other in today's world. The Islamic perspective is so unique that NPR's Robert Siegel discussed the work with the author on the "All Things Considered" program. This interview won the national award for the best radio interview of the year.

Nasr, Seyyed Hossein, *Islamic Science. An Illustrated Study*. This is the first illustrated study of the whole of Islamic science ever undertaken. Basing himself on the Traditional Islamic concept of science and its transmission and classification, the author discusses various branches of the Islamic sciences from cosmology, geography, and other qualitative and descriptive sciences to the mathematical sciences which include arithmetic, algebra, trigonometry geometry, astronomy, and music as well as certain branches of physics. He also presents the history of medicine, pharmacology, alchemy, agriculture and various forms of technology.

Nasr, Seyyed Hossein, *Muhammad: Man of God*. This short study of the life of the Prophet takes the spiritual dimensions into consideration as well as the more factual and historical elements of the life of the person who changed human history.

Siddiqui, Abdul Hameed, *The Life of Muhammad*. This is one of the best biographies on the Prophet in English.

Waheedin, Seyyed, *The Benefactor and the Rightly-Guided*. The approach to the lives of these Muslims is rational and humanistic in relating the progressive and social values which motivated the early Muslim community and its leaders.

GLOSSARY

abd: Servant, bondsman.

adhan (or *azan*): The Islamic call to prayer, either issued from the minaret of a mosque or among a congregation gathers for *salah*.

Ahl al-Kitab: The People of the Scripture those to whom a scripture was revealed by God through the prophets i. e., the Jews and Christians.

al-Ameen: The Trustworthy, a title given to Muhammad before his call to prophethood by the people of Mecca in recognition of his upright character.

al-Bait al-Haram: The Sacred House i. e., the Kabah.

al-ghaib: The "hidden" or "unseen," referring to those aspects of Reality which are beyond the human being's perception sensory capacities or awareness.

Allah: The Arabic name for God.

Allahu *Akbar*: "God is Greater" an oft-repeated phrase among Muslims which occupies a prominent place in *salah*.

al-masjid al-haram: The Sacred Mosque i.e., the Great Mosque in Mecca inside which the Kabah is located.

ameer: Leader, commander or head of a community.

Arafat: A vast, barren plain near Mecca, the scene of one of the major observances of *hajj*.

ar-rooh: The Spirit, a title by which the Angel Gabriel is referred to in the Quran; *rooh al-qudus* and *rooh al-ameen* (the Holy Spirit and the Trustworthy Spirit respectively) are additional Quranic appellation for Gabriel.

ashaduan la ilaha illa Llah wa ashaduanna Muhammadan Rasool Allah (or *abduhu wa rasooluhu*): 'I bear witness that there is no deity except God and I bear witness that Muhammad is the Messenger of God (or His servant and Messenger)," the Islamic *shahadah* or Declaration of Faith.

ash-shahadah: The "witnessed" or "evident." Refers both to (1) the Declaration of Faith or creed of Islam and (2) to the visible or known realm of existence which is accessible to the human being's senses, faculties or awareness.

assalamu alaikam wa rahmatallah: "Peace be on you and God's mercy," a phrase of greeting used by Muslims both in meeting and leave-taking, which is also repeated at the end of every prescribed prayer.

bismillah ar-rahman ar-raheem: In the Name to God, the Merciful, the Compassionate, a phrase with which Muslims begin endeavors or actions, including meals.

chador: The outer garment of the women of Iran, consisting of a long draped cloth covering the head and body.

deen: Religion or way of life.

Dhul-Hijjah: The twelfth month of the Islamic calendar during which the *hajj* and the festival of *eid al-adha* take place annually.

eid al-adha: The festival of sacrifice occurring at the time of the *hajj*.

eid al-fitr: The festival of ending the fast at the conclusion of Ramadan.

fard: Obligatory or required.

fiqh: Islamic jurisprudence.

ghusl: A bath with running water.

hadith: The sayings of the Prophet, often referred to as "the Traditions."

hajj: The pilgrimage to Mecca.

halal: Permissible.

haram: Prohibited.

haya: Shyness, modesty and careful guarding of propriety.

hijab: The covering dress of Muslim women which is required by Islam.

hijrah: The migration of Prophet Muhammad from Mecca to Medina, heralding the foundation of the Islamic society and state.

hudood: Plural of *hadd*; literally, "the limits" imposed by God, including the punishments laid down by Islam for various crimes.

ibadat: Acts of worship such as praying, fasting, *zakah, hajj, dhikr* (the glorification of God) and reading the Quran.

iftar: Ending the fast at sunset.

ihram: In a general sense, a state in which external involvements are prohibited. Specifically, the state of consecration, as well as the dress pertaining to this state, of the pilgrim during *hajj* and *umrah*.

ilah: Deity, i.e., anyone or anything who is worshiped, served and obeyed, to whom ultimate allegiance and devotion are given, and to whom sovereignty and absolute authority are ascribed.

imam: Leader

iman: Deep faith and trust in God

Injeel: The Evangel or Good News, the original Scripture revealed to Jesus by God

Islam: Pronounced Iss-laam (not Iz-lum) In a general sense, submission to God; in the specific sense, the final statement of God's guidance to mankind revealed through Prophet Muhammad.

jihad: Earnest striving or effort, either within oneself, in society or in the world at large, for righteousness and against evil, wrongdoing and oppression

Kabah: The first house for the worship of the One God built on earth, situated in Mecca, Arabia.

Khalifat Rasool Allah: Successor to the Messenger of God, i. e., the caliphs or heads of the Muslim *ummah* and state after the death of the Prophet. The last of the caliphs was deposed in Ottoman Turkey in 1924.

La ilaha illa Llah, Muhammadun rasool Allah: "There is no deity except God, Muhammad is the Messenger of God," the Islamic creed.

lailat al-qadr: The Night of Power during which the first revelation of the Quran was revealed to the Prophet, commemorated annually toward the end of Ramadan.

madhab: school of Islamic jurisprudence or *fiqh*.

mahram: The prohibited degrees of relationship, i. e., those near blood relatives of the opposite sex with whom marriage is prohibited in Islam.

Marwah: One of the two small hills adjacent to the Sacred Mosque in Mecca, the site of *sa i*; one of the rites of *hajj* or *umrah*.

Muharram: The first month of the Islamic calendar.

Muhammedan: A name often used, incorrectly, by non-Muslims for the followers of Islam (Muslims). This term has never been used by Muslims themselves and is totally unacceptable to them, as it implies that they worship or that their religion revolves around the man Muhammad.

mu'min: One who possesses *iman* or deep faith and trust in God.

muslim, Muslim: In a general sense, anyone who submits to God, including all the true prophets of all times. In the more specific sense, one who submits to God by following the religion of Islam. Pronounced Muss-lim, not Muz-lim or Moz-lem.

muttaqeen: Those who possess *taqwa* or consciousness of God.

nabi: Prophet

purdah: A Persian/Urdu word denoting both the covering dress of Muslim women and their not mixing with men outside the family circle

qada wa qadar: The "measure" of what has been ordained by God and His "plan," i. e., the divine decree

qiblah: The direction of Mecca (the Kabah) from any point on the globe.

Qur'an: The divinely-revealed Scripture of Islam. Pronounced Quur-aan, not Koran

rak'at: Unit of *salah*, cycle.

Ramadan: The ninth month of the Islamic Calendar, the Islamic month of fasting.

rasool: A messenger of God; in the technical sense, a prophet who is entrusted with a divinely-revealed scripture.

Safa: One of the two small hills adjacent to the Sacred Mosque in Mecca, related to the performance of *sui*.

sa'i: "Hastening" between the two hillocks of Safa and Marwah, one of the rites of *hajj* and *umrah*.

salah: The prayers or worship prescribed for Muslims five times daily.

salah al-jum'ah: The obligatory Friday congregational worship.

sawm: (or *siyam*): Fasting.

Shari'ah: Literally, "the way"; the code of life of Islam, based on the Quran and the Prophet's *sunnah*.

Shawwal: The tenth month of the Islamic calendar, during which the festival of *eid al-fitr* takes place.

Shi'ah: Those Muslims who adhere to the principle of succession to the leadership of the Muslim *ummah* through the descendants of Ali and Fatimah

shirk: Associating others with God's divinity, either in the form of polytheism or by ascribing authority and sovereignty, or giving one's worship and obedience, to someone or something other than God.

shura: Mutual consultation.

Sunnah: The practice of the Prophet, consisting of what he himself did, recommended or approved of in others.

Sunni: Short for *ahl al-sunnah wa al-jama'ah*, the People of the Sunnah and the Community, i.e., the majority of Muslims.

surah: Chapter of the Quran.

surat al-fateha: The opening chapter of the Quran.

tahajjud: A non-obligatory *salah* which may be observed during the last one-third of the night.

taqwa: Consciousness of God, comprised of love and fear of Him and the desire to merit His pleasure.

taraweeh: *salah*: A special *salah* performed in Ramadan after the last prayer of the day.

tawaf: Circumambulation or encircling the Kabah while praising and supplicating God, one of the essential rites of *hajj* and *umrah*.

Torah: The original Scripture revealed to Moses by God.

tayammum: Dry ablution preceding *salah* which replaces the use of water (*wudu*): when water is not available or its use is likely to be injurious due to illness.

ubudiyat: The state of enslavement or creatureliness of the human being and all the rest of creation in relation to God.

ummah: Community or collectivity.

umrah: The Lesser Pilgrimage.

wudu: Ablution preceding *salah*.

Yathrib: An old name for Medina.

zaboor: The divinely-revealed Scripture given to the Prophet David.

zakah: The obligatory poor-due of Islam.

Zamzam: The well or spring within the compound of the Sacred Mosque in Mecca.

GENERAL INDEX